Hiking
Arizona

by
**Stewart Aitchison and
Bruce Grubbs**

(Formerly *The Hiker's Guide to Arizona*)

FALCON™

Falcon Press® Publishing Co., Inc.,
Helena, Montana

A FALCON GUIDE

Falcon Press is continually expanding its list of recreational guidebooks. All books include detailed descriptions, accurate maps, and all the information necessary for enjoyable trips. You can order extra copies of this book and get information and prices for other Falcon guidebooks by writing Falcon Press, P.O. Box 1718, Helena, MT 59624 or calling toll-free 1-800-582-2665. Also, please ask for a free copy of our current catalog.

All text, maps, and photos by the authors.
Cover photo by Tom Bean.

 Printed on Recycled Paper

CAUTION

Outdoor recreation activities are by their very nature potentially hazardous. All participants in such activities must assume the responsibility for their own actions and safety. The information contained in this guidebook cannot replace sound judgment and good decision– making skills, which help reduce risk exposure, nor does the scope of this book allow for disclosure of all the potential hazards and risks involved in such activities.

Learn as much as possible about the outdoor recreation activities you participate in, prepare for the unexpected, and be safe and cautious. The reward will be a safer and more enjoyable experience.

CONTENTS

HIKING IN ARIZONA—AN INTRODUCTION

HIKING TECHNIQUES AND ETHICS

MAKING IT A SAFE TRIP

THE HIKES

Central Mountains—Mogollon Rim, Mazatzal Mountains, Bradshaw Mountains, White Mountains

Southern and Western deserts—Superstition Mountains, Santa Catalina Mountains, Rincon Mountains, Santa Rita Mountains, Chiricahua Mountains, Hualapai Mountains, Dragoon Mountains, Huachua Mountains, Pinaleno Mountains, Galiuro Mountains, Lower Colorado River

ACKNOWLEDGMENTS

We wish to thank all of you who made this book a reality. Special thanks go out to the hikers who over the years have freely given of their time and knowledge to allow us to explore the wonderful state of Arizona.

It was a tremendous help to receive trail descriptions from Chuck Bame, Tom Bean, Steve Gustafson, Sid Hirsh, Steve Knox, Rudi Lambrechtse, Ken Mahoney, Larry Mutter, John Nelson, Gary Russell, and Bill Williams. Legendary Grand Canyon hiker Harvey Butchart generously loaned us his monumental collection of hiking notes.

Thanks, too, to Dale Shewalter for his description of the Arizona Trail, Dawson Henderson of the Arizona Wilderness Coalition for his essay, and Bruce Babbitt, Arizona's most famous hiker, for writing the Foreword.

Many individuals with the Bureau of Land Management, National Park Service, and United States Forest Service gave generously of their time and knowledge, and we appreciate it.

Last but certainly not least, we thank Bill Schneider, and all the fine folks at Falcon Press for transforming our rough notes into a real guide book.
—*Stewart Aitchison and Bruce Grubbs*

PREFACE

Viewed from a plane, the Arizona landscape looks like a huge relief map. The contours and convolutions of the earth are apparent, with canyons, mountain ranges, mesas, and valleys fitting together. The geologic complexity and immensity of the land is much easier to appreciate. But from a high altitude, the land appears lifeless.

Viewed from a speeding car, the Arizona landscape is constantly changing: from Sonoran desert with its menacing array of spiny plants punctuated by giant saguaro cactus, to gnarly junipers dotting a grass-and-prickly pear plain. The road winds higher, among cool ponderosa pine forests where extinct volcanoes jut skyward. Mysterious twisting canyons, isolated mesa tops, and mountain summits rush by, and only the largest plants are noticeable. Wildlife seems exceptionally sparse—except for frequent and unfortunate road kills.

But traveling on foot, with a backpack filled with necessities and perhaps a few luxuries, we can feel the geology beneath our feet, witness the intricate beauty of a cactus flower, wonder over the life of some ancient cliff dweller, observe the clumsy, comical mating of two desert tortoises, and hear the wild scream of a red-tailed hawk.

Only on foot, close to the land, away from the mechanized world, can we truly appreciate nature and perhaps discover our place in the universe. The trip doesn't have to be an epic two-week-long hike, lugging a sixty-pound backpack on weary shoulders. An afternoon stroll down a flat sandy wash may be sufficient to travel a long way toward understanding and enjoying the natural world.

FOREWORD

My favorite place is Sierra Ancha, the wide mountain. In August, when Phoenix heat is no longer bearable, we leave, driving east past Roosevelt Lake, up a rocky track past the forks of Workman Creek, through damp thickets of mountain locust, columbine, and raspberry into the rain forests that cover Aztec Peak. There the road ends. The trail begins.

We spend the mornings on walks through the dense fir and spruce thickets, pausing to gaze across the ramparts of Pueblo Canyon over the honey-colored desert stretching eastward 3,000 feet below. In the afternoon, cumulus clouds build up and explode in a frenzy of lightning, thunder, and sudden cold rain. Evening is a quiet play of light and shadow. As the clouds break and drift away, a pale moon floats up from the pink, receding desert horizon reaching through the twisted branches of old pine.

This is Arizona! Yet, it is also the silence of stone and brilliant light of the inner Grand Canyon, where human significance shrinks to the vanishing point. It is the rainbow of color in the widest vista of the painted desert. It is the spiraling red waves and cobalt light of the Vermilion Cliffs. It is the Gila woodpecker spinning out of her burrow in the saguaro cactus, then pirouetting in space over the sand and gravel reaches of the Sonoran Desert. And, it is the complete circular vision atop the Kachina Wilderness—knowing that this is home to the beings of the Hopi spiritual path.

In Arizona, there is great beauty just one step in any direction. We have four seasons almost any time of year. We have examples of almost every ecosystem type in America. Your awakening to the natural world can come from just one trip to any of the magical places described in this book.

What the authors have done is to make the first and successive trips more feasible. With lucid prose and clear maps, we have before us one of the finest hiking guides for Arizona to date from two of our foremost adventurers. Because many of the places described here are not heavily traveled, the opportunity for new exploration of lesser known places is enhanced. The opportunity for surprise awaits. Only you can take the first step. Now there is no reason to wait another day!

Bruce Babbitt, Secretary of the Interior

LOCATION OF HIKES

HIKING IN ARIZONA, AN INTRODUCTION

This is obviously a book about hiking in Arizona, but many of you familiar with the state may wonder about some glaring omissions. Where, for example, is a description of the popular Bright Angel Trail in the Grand Canyon? The spectacular Paria Canyon hike is also missing, and the West Fork of Oak Creek?

Indeed, these and many more hikes not included in this guide are wonderful hikes. But the main purpose of *Hiking Arizona* is to provide an overall review of hiking in Arizona and to introduce hikers to lesser-known areas of the state— the entire state, not just its most-publicized hikes. Nevertheless, we have included those deservedly famous hikes like Aravaipa Canyon, which, although quite popular, also feature well-regulated access.

Use this guide book as a starting point to discover your own favorite hikes in the remote corners of the Grand Canyon, Superstition Mountains, Mogollon Rim country, and other wilderness gems of Arizona.

Geology and geography

Imagine yourself high above Arizona, swooping down across Arizona from the north low enough to see mountains, canyons, and forests, yet high enough to see clear across the state, several hundred miles in any direction.

Crossing into Arizona at about the center of the common boundary with Utah, you pass over the southern and western portions of the Colorado Plateau. Though truly a plateau (as opposed to a mountainous region), the Colorado Plateau is anything but flat and featureless. A number of volcanic mountains and uplifts dot the surface, while hundreds of canyons slash deep into sedimentary rocks, draining into a series of master canyons cut by the Colorado River. The river and its canyons so dominate the landscape that the entire Plateau, covering parts of four states, was named after it.

Below you are the lower reaches of Glen Canyon and Lake Powell. To your left, or east, is a fantastic labyrinth of red sandstone canyons, knobs, and fins sprawled around the base of forested, dome-shaped Navajo Mountain. Off to the southeast are the countless red sandstone plateaus and occasional higher forested mesas of the immense Navajo and Hopi Indian reservations, stretching to the base of the Carrizo Mountains along the New Mexico border.

Directly below, the spectacular gorge of Marble Canyon opens to view, sliced through the layer cake geology of the Colorado Plateau by the Colorado River, which is clearly visible at the bottom of the canyon. Marble Canyon widens before you, a fitting prelude to the greatest of all Colorado River canyons, the Grand Canyon. The high, forested Kaibab Plateau lies to the west, and beyond it, the remote Arizona Strip country, that part of Arizona separated from the rest of the state by the Grand Canyon. Here ancient volcanic cones spewed lava which flowed into Grand Canyon and formed dams and lakes dwarfing any man-made reservoir.

Now the expanse of the Grand Canyon unfolds, wandering more than two hundred river-miles to the west and only ending near the southern tip of Nevada. A classic exposition of geologic strata, the canyon clearly shows how ancient mountains have grown—raised by subterranean pressures which move continents like rafts in the world ocean—only to be destroyed by the seemingly modest forces of wind and water. Rock layers show how great oceans and deserts formed in alternation, not once but several times, each depositing their own unique rocks in distinct horizontal beds.

Southward, you pass over fields of lava flows and a landscape marked with numerous cinder cones and volcanic mountains, finally culminating in the alpine San Francisco Peaks, the highest in the state. Off to the southeast, the Colorado Plateau gradually rises and becomes forested with a rich stand of pines. Abruptly the land drops as you pass over the edge of the Mogollon Rim, which recedes east into the distance. The White Mountains, 9,000-11,000 feet high but gentle and rolling, are visible where the rim fades into New Mexico.

The edge of the rim marks the end of the gentler plateau landscape and a transition into the rugged mountain country of central Arizona. A number of deep canyons slash through the Rim, draining into the valleys below. Adjacent mountain ranges, though not high by alpine standards, offer such complex terrain that they are virtual wonderlands of stone, forest, and stream. There are many fine opportunities for backpacking and hiking in this region.

As you continue southward, mountain ranges become lower and farther apart. The city of Phoenix sprawls across a huge desert valley, and the transition to more open terrain is obvious.

To the southwest, the ranges are more desert-like as the general elevation of the land drops. Rugged desert ranges such as the Eagletails and Kofas thrust jagged summits into the sky. To the southeast, the land is generally higher and so are the mountains, reaching 9,000-10,000 feet. Outstanding ranges are the Pinalenos, Chiricahuas, and Galiuros.

This Basin-and-Range topography of alternate mountain ranges and valleys covers the southwestern half of Arizona and large areas of California, Nevada, and Utah. The mountain ranges, some small, some extending a hundred miles or more, trend in a general north-south direction, parallel ranges probably formed by the collision of drifting continental plates which stressed the bedrock. As these stresses increased from the west, the crust of the earth cracked and heaved great blocks of rock upward, often tilting them and dropping the valley floors at the same time. The mountains vary from low, rounded desert hills to alpine peaks with dense forests and permanent streams.

Natural history

Arizona is remarkably rich and diverse in plant and animal life. Habitats range from searing desert to alpine tundra. Annual precipitation can vary from almost none to more than fifty inches. In general the driest areas of the state are the low western and southwestern sections and the wettest regions are the high plateaus and mountains. Arizona typically has two rainy seasons: winter and late summer. At higher elevations (above 5,000 feet) the winter precipitation generally falls as snow. Flagstaff (at 7,000 feet), for example, averages about eighty inches of snow a season. Summer precipitation usually

2

takes the form of afternoon thundershowers which, although generally brief, often result in heavy run-off and flash floods because of the rocky nature of the ground.

The sun shines 85-90 percent of the daytime in Arizona's lower desert regions and only slightly less in higher country. Annual temperature extremes have spanned more than 160 Fahrenheit degrees, from a low of -37 at Maverick to a high of 127 at Parker. Daily fluctuations commonly exceed forty degrees or more, which is characteristic of arid regions. The normally low humidity allows daytime heat to quickly dissipate at night.

Arizona's plants and animals have evolved communities admirably adapted to surviving under these various, often extreme, environmental conditions. Biologists generally define these communities in terms of the dominant type of vegetation.

Arizona contains six major biotic communities. These, in order of descending altitude, are (1) Alpine Tundra (12,670-11,000 feet); (2) Coniferous Forest, including aspen groves (11,000-6,000 feet); (3) Woodlands (7,000-4,000 feet); (4) Chaparral (6,000- 4,000 feet); (5) Grasslands (7,000-4,000 feet); and (5) Deserts (6,000-100 feet). The only major North American biotic community not represented in the state is tropical. In fact, a hike from the summit of the San Francisco Peaks to the bottom of the Grand Canyon, a distance of only eighty miles, is similar in terms of biotic communities to a hike from northern Canada to northern Mexico.

In these six communities are found some 3,370 species of flowering plants, ferns, and fern allies, sixty-four species of fishes, twenty-two species of amphibians, ninety-seven species of reptiles, 434 species of birds, and 138 species of mammals. Arizona has sixty percent of all types of wildlife species found in North America. This of course doesn't include the multitude of insects, arachnids, mosses, lichens, and other living organisms that constitute the rest of the ecosystem. Arizona—considered by many people a vast, lifeless desert—actually has a startling abundance of living, breathing, reproducing plants and creatures.

The protection of this wildlife, plantlife, and natural habitat is perhaps the most urgent reason to set aside wilderness areas in Arizona. In addition to the sheer enjoyment and rejuvenation which many people find in observing nature, useful products such as medicines have been developed from native species. Scientists have only begun to discover the wonders of Arizona's indigenous species.

Arizona people

Arizona's earliest human inhabitants were hunters who arrived at least 11,000 years ago, soon after the retreat of the continental glaciers. Those sheets of ice didn't reach as far south as Arizona, but they did affect the climate of the state, producing cooler and wetter weather. Local glaciers, moreover, did exist at higher elevations—in the San Francisco Peaks near Flagstaff, for example.

Arizona's early hunters stalked mammoth, ground sloth, giant bison, Harrington's mountain goat, tapirs (pig-like animals), camels, and other relics of the Pleistocene Age. But after generations of these hunters and a gradual warming and drying of the climate, such species became extinct. The hunters turned their attention to smaller game such as deer, elk, bighorn, antelope, rabbits, squirrels and other rodents, birds, amphibians, reptiles, fishes, and

3

invertebrates. They also placed a greater emphasis on gathering native plants for food. They had to be opportunists to survive in this harsh land.

Approximately four thousand years ago, maize and squash were introduced to Arizona through trade with other peoples to the south, in Mexico. The hunter-gathers of Arizona gradually became farmers. And as farmers, they tended to stay longer in one place. They didn't have to follow wild herds. Instead they sought out arable land, sowed their seeds, raised their crops, and—in good years—enjoyed bountiful harvests in the fall.

With a more dependable food supply, Arizona's human population slowly began to increase. More people, in turn, engaged in more agriculture. Farming intensified. Three major and distinct Indian cultures developed. People in the southern part of the state, the Hohokam, engineered complex irrigation canals to bring water from the wetter, higher mountains to the desert lowlands. People on the northern plateau, the Anasazi, also farmed but relied mainly on natural precipitation, although they did discover ingenious ways to channel run-off so that the water reached their fields. The Mogollon people, who lived along the central mountain belt, practiced both irrigation and dry farming.

An important addition to the diet of these early Indians occurred about 600-700 A.D., when the bean—a variety very similar to today's pinto bean—was first cultivated. Corn and beans eaten together gave Arizona's early inhabitants a complete source of protein, undoubtedly improving their health and increasing their survival rate. Population boomed.

Life in those days was good. Fields of corn, squash, beans, and cotton grew where cactus or juniper had been. Large villages were constructed of mud, stone, and logs. Indians, living to the ripe old age of thirty or even thirty-five, produced beautiful pottery and developed elaborate religous ceremonies to insure the coming of rain and good fortune.

Then, after six or seven centuries of prosperity, people in the north began having difficulties and started abandoning their homes. What caused their displacement is still not fully understood, but probably involved a combination of extensive drought, overuse of natural resources, overpopulation, and perhaps disease and warfare. By the mid-1400s, people along the Mogollon Rim and southern deserts had also left their villages.

Some of these early peoples moved out of the Arizona region entirely, while others resumed hunting and gathering. A few, such as the Hopi, found locations favorable to their dry-farming methods and continued their agricultural tradition. Also about this same time, new peoples moved into the area, including the Navajo and Apache, primarily nomadic hunting and gathering groups.

In the early 1500s, the first non-Indians arrived upon the scene—Spanish conquistadors looking for gold and other treasures. The first non-Indian to step on Arizona soil was Estevan, a black Moor, who was guiding Fray Marcos de Niza to find legendary golden cities. Soon behind them came the Spanish Fathers looking for heathen souls to save.

Some native American groups fared better than others at repelling the Spanish invasion. But between 1821 and 1854, Arizona fell under Mexican rule, and by the mid-1850s more intruders were coming—this time American fur trappers, such as James Ohio Pattie, Jedediah Smith, Bill Williams, Pauline Weaver, and Kit Carson. They were followed a few years later by prospectors, ranchers, and settlers.

Conflict erupted as these different people fought over Arizona's limited resources. By the end of the nineteenth century, the Old West was quickly becoming a memory as more territory was settled and new conflicts of interest arose. On Valentine's Day, 1912, Arizona became a state.

Today, Arizona is one of the fastest-growing states. Many retired people seeking refuge from the northern states' severe winters are flocking to the sunny Southwest. The central and southern areas of the state are quickly becoming urbanized and industrialized. Outdoor recreation continues to grow. Only wise planning today will insure that Arizonans have recreational lands tomorrow. □

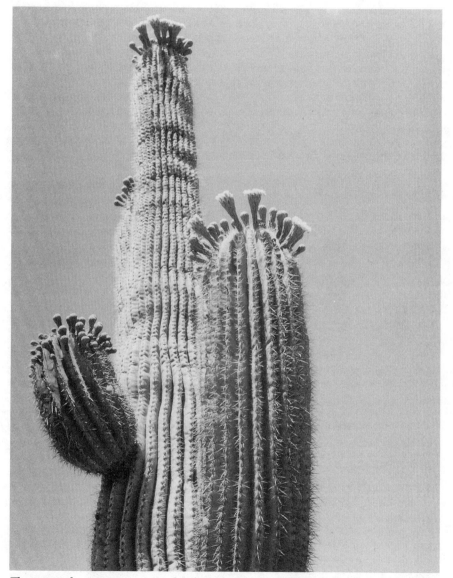

The spectacular saguaro cactus is often found in the Arizona desert backcountry. Backcountry travelers should be aware that it is illegal to remove the saguaro from its natural habitat.

HIKING TECHNIQUES AND ETHICS

Touching the land lightly

The American wilderness belongs to all Americans. All of us have the right to enjoy the wilderness, but with that right comes responsibility to take care of the backcountry. Vehicle campers and users of organized recreation areas have come to expect that land managers and forest rangers will maintain recreation sites and clean up after them, but no such services are possible in wilderness areas. Each wilderness user must first of all clean up after himself or herself, and secondly clean up after others who have been careless.

Most wilderness messes appear to be made by people who do not realize how precious and limited wilderness is. Thinking it will be years before anyone passes by again, they leave orange peels strewn about their rest stops, build new campfire rings in campsites already dotted with campfire rings, and try to burn aluminum food packages or bury garbage. Meanwhile another

If you build a campfire, be sure to return the site to its natural condition before leaving. The easiest way is to initially dig a small fire pit into mineral soil. When you are breaking camp, mix the ashes with dirt and water. Make sure the fire is dead out, then cover it with soil and scatter any fire-blackened rocks. Better still, cook on a backpacker's stove and use a candle with foil windbreak as a cheery campfire substitute. Bruce Grubbs group of hikers is a few days or hours behind, hungry eyes watch from the brush, and aluminum sparkles on the ground as it will for hundreds of years. The golden rule of wilderness—"Leave it the same way you would like to find it"—has been violated again.

Never litter the trail or countryside. Most litter along trails in Arizona is probably accidental, except near heavily populated areas, and many hikers pick up litter when they find it, especially on day hikes or toward the end of multi-day trips. When setting up camp, note the appearance of the site and resolve to leave it looking as good or better. In particular, avoid excavating

Some fires are caused by lightning, including this conflagration near the Kachina Peaks Wilderness Area. Unfortunately, however, many other fires are the result of human carelessness. Since fire restrictions may be imposed on national forests after long dry spells, check with the local ranger before building fires. Stewart Aitchison tent ditches or large-scale earth-moving to create sleeping sites. Look for areas of sand or pine needles which are naturally smooth and comfortable, instead of digging away at imbedded rocks. With a good sleeping pad, even slabs of rock make excellent campsites.

Campfires account for much of the scarring of campsites. In many heavily used areas, campfires have been permanently prohibited, and in others are prohibited in summer and fall due to the danger of wildfire. Follow such restrictions to the letter. In areas where fires are allowed, you still should not build one if the site is short on firewood or if the wind is blowing. When you do build a fire, avoid building elaborate fire rings and scarring rocks and boulders. Find a site from which it is unlikely the fire can spread, in soft sand or soil. Dig a shallow hole, heaping dirt around the edges. Keep your fire small, and when you leave, fill in the hole with the loose dirt. Do a careful job, and a patch of disturbed soil or sand will be the only evidence you leave behind.

Increasing contamination of wilderness water supplies is a consequence of heavy backcountry use, yet most problems can be prevented with a little common sense. Always answer the call of nature at least 100 yards from any open water, and farther if possible. Dig a hole 4-8 inches deep and bury everything carefully when you are finished. Some people carry a plastic garden trowel to make digging easier.

Preserving our archaeological and historical heritage

Arizona is fortunate to have some of the best-preserved prehistoric structures and artifacts in the world. Unfortunately about ninety percent of the known sites have been vandalized to some degree. Disturbing archaeological sites and artifacts does not simply lessen their scientific value—such activity is essentially grave-robbing.

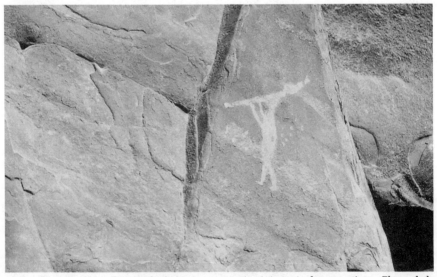

Indian pictographs and petroglyphs are common in Arizona's desert regions. Please help preserve them by not touching them, since the oils in your skin may affect the pigments. Also, sometimes the rock is so friable that a piece may crumble at the slightest touch, and with it a part of history. Stewart Aitchison

Two federal laws, the Antiquities Act and the Archaeological Resources Protection Act, forbid removal or destruction of archaeological artifacts and ruins on federal land. An Arizona State Antiquities Act provides similar protection on state lands. Failure to comply with these laws can result in stiff fines and imprisonment. Any vandalism should be immediately reported to the nearest federal or state resource office.

About the maps

Each hike in *Hiking Arizona* is accompanied by a sketch map showing the access road and specific trails mentioned in the hike description. This map should be used only as a general guide, indicating the length and type of hike under discussion. More detailed maps are useful for many hikes described in this book.

One type of more detailed map is the topographic map, or quad, published by the U.S. Geological Survey. These maps come in two basic series, the 7.5-minute and 15-minute quads. The 15-minute quads are generally older maps, sometimes outdated. All newer mapping is being done in the more detailed 7.5-minute series, and these maps show recent roads, trails, and other man-made features. Both series are quite accurate in depicting terrain, which normally does not change significantly. For some areas both 7.5- and 15-minute maps may be available, but generally only one or the other series applies to a specific hike.

A second type of detailed map useful for hikes described here is the National Forest and Wilderness map, published by the U.S. Forest Service. Forest Service maps do not show topography, but are updated more often than topographic maps. In addition, roads are more clearly classified as maintained, primitive,

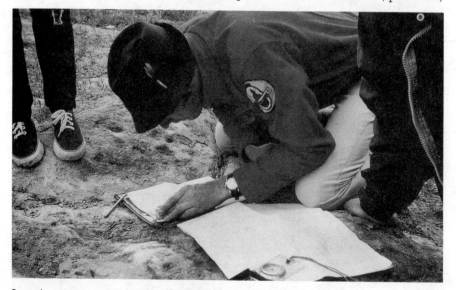

Learning to use maps is not only fun but essential when exploring much of Arizona's backcountry. Trails are often faint and hard to follow, easy to confuse with livestock and game trails. Some of the state's best wild places can only be reached by cross-country travel with map and compass. Practice map reading by obtaining a U.S. Geological Survey topographic map of an area you are already familiar with, such as your hometown. Bruce Grubbs or four-wheel-drive roads. Forest road and trail numbers are also shown on these maps, and on Forest Service signs, making it easier to find the trailhead.

Some wilderness maps have been published by the Forest Service. These are based on topographic maps, and the Forest Service has added more up-to-date road and trail information. Where these maps exist, they are very useful. However, they normally don't show the detail that a USGS quad does.

A third type of detailed map mentioned in some descriptions of southern Arizona hikes is published by the Southern Arizona Hi king Club and is available in bookstores and hiking shops in Tucson. These maps are USGS quads with trails marked on them. The re are four currently available: Catalinas, Rincons, Santa Ritas, and Chiricahuas.

Learning to read maps is not only fun but, in many cases, also essential in keeping yourself from getting lost. The trail descriptions in *Hiking Arizona* are brief and cannot substitute for good map-reading skills. More-over, maps not only make our suggested hikes easier to follow, but they also allow you to plan your own original adventures.

MAP LEGEND

Interstate	(00)	Trailhead	(P)
U.S. Highway	(00)	Trail	----→
State Highway	(000)	River, Creek, Drainage	
Forest Road	[0000]	Drainage	
Paved Road		Springs	♂
Dirt Road		Lakes	
Jeep Road			
Bridge		Depression	
Parking	**P.**	Peak & Elevation	X 0000'
Tunnel		Rim	
Corral			
Building	■		
Ranger Station		NORTH	
Campground	△	One Mile	
Tank		Direction Orientation Symbol, and Map Scale, Trail Location	

MAKING IT A SAFE TRIP

Backcountry Safety

Backpacking and hiking are by nature are casual and relaxed sports. However, it is important to remember that the wilderness is totally indifferent to the presence of human visitors. While there are no forces seeking to harm hikers, there are none seeking to help them, either. In any kind of wilderness emergency—whether snakebite, a sudden snowstorm, or scorching heat—you are entirely on your own. Even if companions can go for help in an emergency, hours or days may pass before rescuers arrive.

Backcountry safety is largely a matter of common sense. Avoid pushing yourself or members of your party beyond their abilities. Most twisted ankles and broken bones occur because someone was rushing to reach a goal or pushing a slow hiker. Any group can travel safely only as fast as its slowest member.

Arizona trails such as this one in Whitmore Canyon in western Grand Canyon can be long, steep, dry, and isolated. Never hike alone. Stewart Aitchison

Plan your trip carefully, allowing extra time to reach each day's campsite (or to return to the car on a day hike). You may be distracted by a side hike or want to spend extra time on a mountain top. If something goes wrong, such as a bad blister, you will have time to take care of the problem. Plan for events such as sudden snowstorms, and consider exit routes where you can abort the trip early if needed.

Carry a first aid kit and know how to use it. Take a first aid course!

Dying of thirst

The availability of water governs most backpack trips in Arizona. Most people plan their hikes so that there is water at each campsite and lunch stop and carry at least two quarts of water. Except during the winter, two quarts is usually a safe minimum, but in hotter weather or when water sources are uncertain, the safe minimum may be four to eight quarts per person per day.

Although topographic and forest maps show springs and running streams, do not count on the water actually being there unless you have a reliable source of information or personal experience which indicates so. Many springs and streams dry up after long dry periods of weather. Be aware of recent weather and precipitation, and carry enough water to see you through to the next water source if one happens to be dry.

Keep in mind that it is unnecessary to camp at a water source. Many dry camps are more pleasant than overused, trampled campsites near springs. Besides, your presence may prevent wildlife from coming for a drink—which could be particularly critical during the dry summer months.

There are a number of reliable collapsible water containers on the market. With one of these a hiker can carry enough water from the last spring of the day to last through the night and into the next day, until reaching another water source. And hikers who are not restricted to campsites with water can

A few of Arizona's desert canyons are blessed with permanent streams but most are not. Carry plenty of water and purify any water that you drink from natural sources. Bruce Grubbs

choose from a spectacular variety of fine campsites—mountaintops, open ridges, and forested glades.

Can I drink it?

No, you can't. It's sad but true that most wilderness water sources are no longer safe to drink. The exceptions are isolated springs and water flowing directly from a fresh snowfield. Increased human use has contaminated most other water sources, and many have been polluted by domestic cattle or wildlife.

Giardiasis, an often-severe gastrointestinal infection caused by a protozoic parasite, has received much attention in the past few years. Land management agencies and backpackers alike have voiced a great deal of concern over the problem. It now seems clear that the protozoa causing Giardiasis is naturally present in many water supplies, including those of many cities, but is spread to wilderness areas by mammals, including man. Not all people are affected, but for those who are, the symptoms can be incapacitating.

Iodine tablets such as Globaline or Potable Agua will kill most organisms in water, including *Giardia lamblia* and its cysts. Use one tablet per quart (two if the water is contaminated with decaying organic matter such as leaves), and allow the water to stand for ten minutes (twenty minutes if the water is very cold). According to the third edition of *Medicine for Mountaineering*, even resistant *Giardia* cysts are killed by the concentration of iodine released by these tablets. The iodine tablets must be kept sealed in their original container, however, since any moisture will release the iodine and destroy their effectiveness.

Water filters can also be used for purification, but practical filters require a pump for a reasonable output of water and, until recently, seemed too heavy

The floor of Tsegi Canyon on the Navajo Indian Reservation features easy walking, thanks to horizontal beds of sedimentary rocks which occasionally make natural walkways. Stewart Aitchison

and expensive for backpacking. Newer, lighter designs are becoming more available, however. Chlorine tablets are less effective on wilderness water sources because of organic matter in the water which is removed in city water systems.

Freezing to death

It may seem strange to talk about hypothermia in a state as hot as Arizona, but much outdoor recreation in the state takes place in higher areas or during cooler times of the year. Especially in winter and early spring, sudden storms can drop snow on deserts as low as 2,000 feet and several feet of snow can accumulate at higher elevations. Snow is possible between October and May above 5,000 feet and anytime of the year above 9,000 feet, and a number of hikers who were unprepared for such conditions have died.

Before leaving on your trip, get the immediate and long-range weather forecasts. Delay or reschedule your trip if a major winter sorm is forecast. Plan alternate routes and escape routes on longer trips. Learn to read weather from the wind and the sky. An experienced hiker can predict the weather surprisingly well from just these natural signs, and rarely does an approaching storm arrive without some warnings signs.

Learn, too, the symptoms of hypothermia and how to prevent it. With modern clothing and by layering that clothing, it is possible to hike in inclement weather with a considerable margin of safety.

Hiking with children

More and more hikers are heading to the wilderness with their children. Enjoying nature with kids is a simple, inexpensive way to spend time as a family.

Infants must be carried and toddlers can't go very far under their own power, but hiking possibilities are only limited by the parents' imagination (and strength!).

By her first birthday, my daughter Kate had been up Kendrick Peak (Hike 47), Mount Baldy (Hike 60), experienced three Grand Canyon trails, Pima Canyon (Hike 94), Romero Canyon (Hike 93), and Strawberry Crater (Hike 52) to name a few. These were all day-hikes which greatly simplified logistics especially since I often carry lots of camera gear.

For infants, you will need some kind of chest carrier such as those made by Snugglie. Once a child can comfortably support his or her head and sit up, then a backpack/child carrier is much more enjoyable for parent and passenger. Many different brands are available these days. Look for one that has well-padded shoulder straps, waistbelt, and child's seat. A good pack can be adjusted to fit different sized parents and kids, and has a good restraining strap system so that the little one cannot climb out unnoticed.

Food—keep it simple. Take things that you know your child likes. A back-country trip is no place to introduce new foods. Besides the possibility of being rejected, a new food may create stomache problems, and who needs to be changing diapers every few minutes when you're ten miles from the trailhead.

And speaking of diapers, disposable ones are handier than cloth ones on a hike. But remember, you must pack them out. There are biodegradable diapers now available, but still these should not be left in the backcountry since the decomposition process is relatively slow.

Sun—Sunscreen is a necessity here in the sunny Southwest. Check with your doctor for a recommended type and then be sure to use it. If it's not too hot, dress the little one in long sleeves and long pants. And don't forget that feet and hands can easily burn, too. A brimmed or "Foreign Legion"-style hat is a must.

Cold & Heat—Babies and young children are much more vulnerable to extremes in temperature. Take a first aid course (a good idea whether you're a parent or not) and know the signs and treatment of heat-related problems, hypothermia, and frostbite.

Protecting your valuables

When leaving your vehicle at a trailhead, make sure that valuables are out of sight, preferably locked in the trunk. Don't tempt someone to break into your car. Ideally, leave nothing behind in the car and have a worry free hike.

When entering narrow canyons, be aware of the potential for rain and sudden run-off to create a raging flash flood. Remember that a storm which is far out of sight upstream while you hike under cloudless skies may nevertheless pose a life-threatening hazard. Never camp in the bottom of a dry wash. Bruce Grubbs

THE HIKES

These hikes offer a variety of landscapes, difficulty, and length. Most can be day trips for anyone in good physical condition, many can be made into longer backpacks, and several are epic adventures for the hardy and prepared. Since trail conditions do change and roads to trailheads are occasionally closed or re-routed, it is always a good idea to check with the agency listed under "For more information" before planning a trip.

A word about difficulty: Our ratings system for the degree of difficulty of these hikes is, of course, subjective. The difficulty of a particular hike can be influenced by much more than the trail itself—weather, for instance, or the physical condition of the hiker. Yet even generalizations about difficulty can be valuable for hikers unfamiliar with a particular trail, and so *Hiking Arizona* ranks hikes as easy, moderate, or difficult. An easy hike has little elevation gain or loss, is relatively short, and requires a minimum of map-reading skill. A moderate hike has significant elevation gain or loss, is longer or requires more time, may include sections of cross-country travel, and basic map-reading skills are helpful. A difficult hike either (1) has elevation gains or losses of several thousand feet or more, (2) entails hiking eight miles or more per day, and/or (3) requires a advanced topographic map-reading skills.

There are, of course, many other hiking possibilities in addition to those included in *Hiking Arizona,* and part of the fun of hiking is discovering your own favorite places. After gaining some experience on these trails, study topographic and Forest Service maps, join a local hiking club, and plan your own adventures. Arizona's wild places are waiting. Happy Trails!

THE ARIZONA TRAIL

A topographical map of Arizona reveals a corridor of high country that trends north and south from the Utah border to Mexico. A project is underway to develop an "Arizona Trail" that will allow foot and horse travelers to traverse the length of the state through this natural corridor.

During the summer of 1985, Dale Shewalter, Flagstaff teacher and hiking enthusiast, walked the length of Arizona in twenty-one days and became the main force behind the creation of the Arizona Trail.

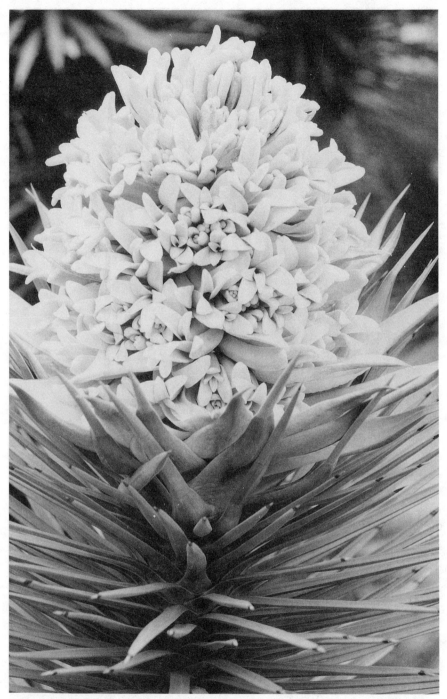

Scattered around the base of the Beaver Dam Mountains are stands of Joshua trees, members of the lily family. The striking bloom is pollinated only by the yucca moth, which in turn depends upon the plant to provide a nesting place and food for the moth's caterpillars—a perfect example of a symbiotic relationship. Stewart Aitchison

As of 1996, more than 300 miles of the proposed 750-mile-long Arizona Trail were signed and open to the public. The goal is to complete the trail border to border by the year 2000. Individuals and groups can be helpful by participating in trail construction and maintenance, publicity, fund raising, education, research, and stewardship of the trail corridor and the affected biological, historic, and cultural resources. For more information, contact the Arizona Trail Association, P.O. Box 36736, Phoenix, AZ 85067.

For hiking information and maps regarding the portions of the trail now open, contact the Arizona Trail Steward, Arizona State Parks, 1300 W. Washington, Phoenix, AZ 85007; (602) 542-4662.

NORTHERN PLATEAU

Overview

This section of Arizona is part of the larger Colorado Plateau, a remarkable geologic province that covers parts of four states. The plateau is characterized by being on average a mile above sea level, composed of horizontal layers of colorful sedimentary rock, and carved into a fantasyland of canyons, mesas and buttes. Hiking is possible year-round but extreme cold and heavy snows are possible from November through March, especially at the higher elevations. Lower canyons can be quite hot during the summer. Most of the northeast portion of northern plateau is Navajo and Hopi Reservation and for the most part closed to hikers. Contact local tribal headquarters for the latest regulations.

HIKE 1 _PARSONS TRAIL_

General description: A day hike into the lower end of Sycamore Canyon Wilderness Area.
General location: About nine miles north of Cottonwood.
Maps: 7.5-minute, Sycamore Basin 7.5-minute USGS quads; Coconino National Forest map.
Difficulty: Easy.
Length: four miles one way.
Elevation: 3,772 to 3,550 feet.
Special attractions: A lovely riparian canyon that attracts many birds during the spring and summer.
Water availability: Sycamore Creek and Parsons Spring
Best season: All year.
For more information: Sedona Ranger District, P.O. Box 300, Sedona, AZ 86336; (520) 282-4119.
Permit: None

The hike: Drive Highway 89A west through Cottonwood to the Tuzigoot National Monument turn-off. Take the turn-off, cross the Verde River Bridge, and turn left onto Forest Road 131. This road follows the Verde River to Duff Flat. Continue on Forest rest Road 131 to the parking area at the trailhead. From the Verde Bridge to the trailhead is about eleven miles.

The trail drops rather steeply for about 200 vertical feet and then follows Sycamore Creek upstream in the canyon. The stream runs year round from Parsons Springs to its junction with the Verde River. Two crossings of the creek are necessary along the trail. These are normally no problem, except during early spring when snow melt from the high country raises the creek level. Large cottonwoods and sycamores shade the route. Water from the creek or several springs should be treated before drinking.

Camping is prohibited from the trailhead to Parsons Spring in order to protect the sensitive riparian or streamside habitat. Camping is allowed north of the spring in the canyon.—_Coconino National Forest._

HIKE 2 _DOE MOUNTAIN TRAIL_

General description: A short day hike in the Red Rock Country.
General location: About five miles northwest of Sedona.
Maps: Wilson Mountain 7.5-minute USGS quad; Coconino National Forest map.
Difficulty: Moderate.
Length: One mile round trip.
Elevation: 4,700 to 5,067 feet.
Special attractions: Great views of an exceptionally colorful stretch of the Mogollon Rim and of the Verde Valley.

NORTH

Canyon

Parsons
Springs

Sycamore

Sycamore Creek

Packard
Trail

Summers
Spring

Verde

P

X 3772'

131

River

One Mile

Water availability: None
Best season: Spring, winter, or fall
For more information: Sedona Ranger District, P.O. Box 300, Sedona, AZ 86336; (520) 282-4119.
Permit: None
Wilderness status: None.

The hike: From West Sedona, take the paved Dry Creek Road north. After about two miles, the paved road changes its name to Boynton Pass Road. At the T-intersection, turn left onto the dirt road and continue about 1.5 miles to Boynton Pass. To your left rises the small mesa known as Doe Mountain. Drive slowly and about mid-way past Doe Mountain, you should see a signed trailhead on your left (southeast). There is a small parking area on your right (northwest).

The Doe Mountain trail climbs to the top in about a half mile and provides lovely vistas of the Mogollon Rim and Verde Valley.—*Stewart Aitchison*

HIKE 2 *DOE MOUNTAIN TRAIL*

HIKE 3 *WILSON MOUNTAIN TRAIL*

General description: A day hike or longer into the Red Rock-Secret Mountain Wilderness Area.

General location: About one mile north of Sedona.

Maps: Wilson Mtn. 7.5-minute, Munds Park 7.5-minute USGS quads; Coconino National Forest map.

Difficulty: Difficult

Length: 4.6 miles one way.

Elevation: 4,520 to 6,900 feet.

Special attractions: Vistas of the Sedona-Red Rock Country.

Water availability: None

Best season: Spring and fall

For more information: Sedona Ranger District, P.O. Box 300, Sedona, AZ 86336; (520) 282-4119.

Permit: None

The hike: This trail can be hiked in a long day with an early start. There is a short steep stretch just below the First Bench and another one from First Bench to the mountain top. Shade is available most of the way, but it can be a long hot walk up the south slopes during warm weather. To find the trailhead, drive north out of Sedona on Highway 89A a couple miles and cross Midgley Bridge. There is parking at the east end of the bridge. Please don't block the gate. Two signed trails begin here: the Wilson Mountain and Wilson Canyon.

The Wilson Mountain trail immediately begins to climb the hillside through lovely Arizona cypress woodland. As the trail gains elevation, you are treated to scenic views of Oak Creek Canyon, Sedona, and the Verde Valley. The cypress is replaced by juniper, pinyon pines, and chaparral. Near the summit, you enter ponderosa pine forest interpersed with small meadows. The trail continues across the summit plateau to overlooks into the Dry Creek Basin or you can walk cross-country to the southern edge of Wilson Mountain for a spectacular look at the Red Rock Country.

Reportedly, the trail originated from the practice of running horses up and down the mountain for grazing purposes. The mount mountain, trail, and canyon were named after Richard Wilson who was killed by a grizzly bear in Wilson Canyon in 1885.—*Coconino National Forest.*

HIKE 4 *WILSON CANYON TRAIL*

General description: A short day hike into the Red Rock—Secret Mountain Wilderness Area.

General location: About 1 mile north of Sedona.

Maps: Wilson Mtn. 7.5-minute USGS quad; Coconino National Forest map.

Difficulty: Easy

Length: Up to one mile one way.

WILSON MOUNTAIN TRAIL
WILSON CANYON TRAIL

One Mile

WILSON MOUNTIAN

X 6900'

Encinoso
Picnic Area

North Wilson Trail

Oak Creek Canyon

Wilson Mtn. Trail

Wilson Canyon Trail

89A

Steamboat Rock

4520'

P

Midgley Bridge

NORTH

Sedona

Elevation: 4,520 to 4,900 feet.

Special attractions: Relict stands of Arizona cypress bounded by soaring cliffs of sandstone.

Water availability: None

Best season: All year.

For more information: Sedona Ranger District, P.O. Box 300, Sedona, AZ 86336; (520) 282-4119.

Permit: None

The hike: This trail begins at the east end of Midgley Bridge just a couple miles north of Sedona on Highway 89A. The Wilson Mountain Trail immediately starts up the hill; whereas the Wilson Canyon Trail stays fairly level and initially follows an old jeep road.

The trail winds through beautiful Arizona cypress stands beneath towering red and buff sandstone buttes and cliffs. Old trails branching off may be confusing but the main route is always near the canyon bottom.—*Coconino National Forest.*

Woods Canyon in the Munds Mountain Wilderness. Stewart Aitchison

HIKE 5 *WOODS CANYON*

General description: An overnight or longer backpack into the Munds Mountain Wilderness Area.
General location: About five miles southeast of Sedona.
Maps: Munds Mountain 7.5-minute USGS quad; Coconino National Forest map.
Difficulty: Moderate.
Length: About fifteen miles one way.
Elevation: 6,400 to 4,000 feet.
Special attractions: Swimming holes, abundant wildlife.
Water availability: Pools and short sections of flowing water along most of the canyon bottom. May dry up entirely in extremely dry years.
Best season: Spring and fall.

HIKE 5 *WOODS CANYON*

For more information: Sedona Ranger District, P.O. Box 300, Sedona, AZ 86336; (520) 282-4119.
Permit: None.

The hike: To hike the length of Woods Canyon, take the Rocky Park exit off of Interstate seventeen about thirty miles south of Flagstaff.

In a high clearance vehicle follow the rough dirt road that leads to Robbers Roost, an abandoned cabin. A game trail, which s seems heavily used by deer and elk, heads west through the forest and eventually to a large open area. In the distance to the s southwest, you can see a major side canyon coming into Woods Canyon. Aim for the rim overlooking the junction of these two canyons. A brushy but passable route can be found to the large pool of water on the canyon floor. It is possible to drop directly into Woods Canyon from Robbers Roost but be prepared for possible wading and bushwhacking. Entering the major side canyon closer to its head is also possible but watch out for abundant poison ivy in the canyon bottom.

Once you are in Woods Canyon, the route is simply down the canyon floor. Most of the way you will be hopping from one basalt boulder to the next. There are some nice narrows where the Coconino Sandstone makes its appearance. Depending on the time of year and whether or not there has been a lot of precipitation, you may encounter several pools that require wading or even swim swimming. On one May hike after a relatively dry spring, we only had to wade twice and managed to climb around an otherwise deep pool.

One of the prettiest places is in the upper canyon where red sandstone ledges overlook deep, clear swimming holes. While hiking downstream, the vegetation along the creek gradually changes from ponderosa pine to sycamores, box elder, and other dedeciduous trees. Elk and black bear sign was noted throughout the canyon.—*Stewart Aitchison*

HIKE 6 *RARICK CANYON*

General description: A one-way hike, requiring a car shuttle, in Rarick Canyon and Red Tank Draw near the Wet Beaver Wilderness Area.
General location: Just east of I-17, between Stoneman Lake Road and Forest Road 618.
Maps: Munds Mountain 7.5-minute, Casner Butte 7.5-minute USGS quads; Coconino National Forest map.
Difficulty: Moderate.
Length: Seven miles.
Elevation: 5,325 to 4,040 feet.
Special attractions: Isolated area, yet accessible by paved roads, prehistoric petroglyphs, large pools.
Water availability: Seasonal stream; some large pools.
Best season: Spring, fall or winter.
For more information: Beaver Creek Ranger Station, H.C. 64, Box 240, Rimrock, AZ 86335; (520) 567-4501.
Permit: None.
Wilderness status: None.

The hike: After leaving a vehicle at the gauging station in lower Red Tank Draw reached by Forest Road 689, go north on I-17 and park at the wide area just east of the Stoneman Lake Road Exit.

Cross the fence and walk east along the abandoned road until you meet Forest Road 213. Proceed straight ahead, across the road and work your way down the brushy slope into Rarick Canyon.

Once in the bottom of the canyon, the brush thins out and you soon come to a series of small water pockets in the sculptured basalt. In this upper section of the canyon, you may spot a gray fox or a herd of javelina.

Following the twists and turns of the canyon for a few miles, you will reach the lip of a twenty-foot fall with a large pool at the bottom. You can climb around either side, but the right (west) side is probably less brushy.

A few more miles of boulder-hopping will bring you to the junction with Mullican Canyon. After another mile, start to look for a trail on the left (east) side of the canyon. This trail begins about where a side canyon comes down from Rays Tank to the east. The trail may be hard to follow since flooding in 1993 rolled tons of basalt boulders along the canyon bottom. Just make your way the best you can along the floor of the canyon.

Before making the short climb up the road to the west to Forest Road 689 and your vehicle, go a few hundred yards below the gauging station to see petroglyphs on both sides of the draw.

In the fall the sycamore trees in the lower portion of the canyon are strikingly beautiful.—*Chuck Bame*

HIKE 7 *APACHE MAID TRAIL*

General description: A day-hike or longer, partly in Wet Beaver Wilderness Area.

General location: About 2.5 miles east of the Sedona Exit on Interstate 17.

Maps: Casner Butte 7.5-minute, Apache Maid Mountain 7.5-minute USGS quads; Coconino National Forest map.

Difficulty: Moderate.

Length: About 4.5 miles to the canyon rim; 9.5 miles one-way to Apache Maid Mountain.

Elevation: 4,040 to 5,200 feet at the rim.

Special attractions: Spectacular, rugged canyon, great vistas.

Water availability: None.

Best season: Spring and fall.

For more information: Beaver Creek Ranger Station, H.C. 64, Box 240, Rimrock, AZ 86335; (520) 567-4501.

Permit: None.

The hike: From I-17 turn east on FR 618 at the Sedona Interchange. Drive approximately two miles and turn left onto Forest Road 618A. Continue .25 mile to the Bell trailhead at the end of the road. About two miles down the Bell Trail, you come to an unsigned fork. The left fork, the Apache Maid Trail, climbs away from Wet Beaver Creek to the saddle between Casner Butte and the canyon rim. Another half-mile as you crest the rim, you leave the wilderness area. This is a good turn-around point for day-hikers.

The hike up offers spectacular views of Wet Beaver and the surrounding terrain. Once outside the wilderness, you enter a mostly level juniper woodland. The trail becomes indistinct and hard to follow but look for rock cairns and posts that mark the route. Antelope and white-tailed deer may be encountered. It is possible to continue a couple more miles to Apache Maid Tanks. Here the trail becomes a four-wheel drive road that continues to Forest Road 620 at Apache Maid Mountain, but by far the most scenic section of trail lies within the canyon.—*Stewart Aitchison*

HIKE 8 *WET BEAVER CREEK*

General description: A three day or longer loop backpack, swim, and wade in the Wet Beaver Wilderness Area.
General location: About 2.5 miles east of the Sedona exit on Interstate 17.
Maps: Casner Butte 7.5-minute, Apache Maid Mountain 7.5-minute USGS quads; Coconino National Forest map.
Difficulty: Difficult.
Length: About twenty-two miles round trip.
Elevation: 4,040 to 6,000 feet.

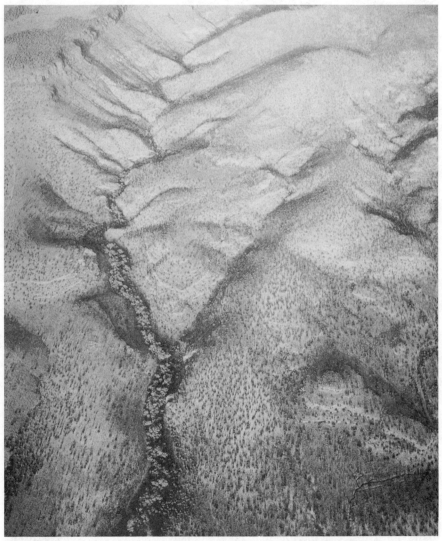

The Wet Beaver Wilderness in the Coconino National Forest. Stewart Aitchison

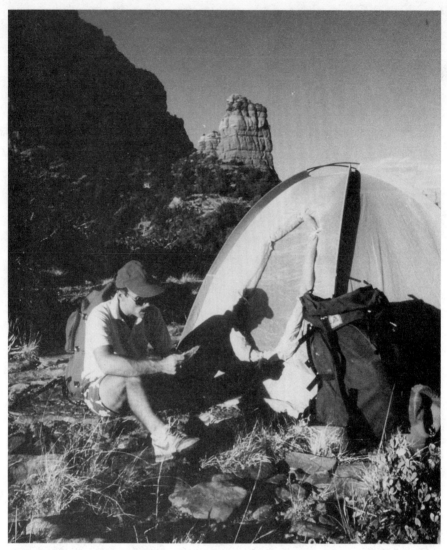

A picturesque campsite in the Coconino National Forest. Stewart Aitchison

Special attractions: Little-visited canyon, stunning scenery.
Water availability: Only along creek.
Best season: May through August.
For more information: Beaver Creek Ranger District, HC 64 Box 240, Rimrock, AZ 86335; (520) 567-4501.
Permit: None:

The hike: For the adventurous, experienced hiker, traversing the length of the Wet Beaver Wilderness Area offers up many challenges.

One possible trip involves first hiking up the Apache Maid Trail (Hike 7) to the rim. Travel east passing to the north of Hog Hill to the head of Waldroup Canyon. In descending Waldroup Canyon, you will encounter seven dry waterfalls that you must climb down. A 40-foot section of ½'' nylon rope is handy for protection. When you reach the floor of Wet Beaver, you are above the headwater springs so the streambed is usually dry. Downstream about 0.5 mile are the main springs that feed Wet Beaver Creek.

To reach Bell Crossing, not far from the Apache Maid trailhead, you will have to swim about twenty pools and wade twice that many. A small inflatable raft or air mattress may be handy for floating your pack. The trip can be made in two days but three or more is better.

A walking stick may be useful to avoid falls on the slick creek bottom. If at all possible, camp away from the creek to lessen impact. Please practice ''no trace'' camping.—*Coconino National Forest.* □

HIKES 9 & 10 *BLODGETT BASIN LOOP TRAIL*
WALKER BASIN TRAIL

HIKE 9 *BLODGETT BASIN WEST CLEAR CREEK LOOP TRAIL*

General description: A little used loop trail in the West Clear Creek Wilderness Area.

General location: About nine miles east of Camp Verde.

Maps: Walker Mtn. 7.5-minute, Buckhorn Mtn. 7.5-minute USGS quads; Coconino National Forest map.

Difficulty: Moderate.

Length: About twelve miles round trip.

Elevation: 5,780 to 3,700 feet.

Special attractions: Rich riparian area, excellent bird watching, fishing, and swimming.

Water availability: West Clear Creek is permanent but should be treated before drinking.

Best season: Spring through fall.

For more information: Beaver Creek Ranger Station, H.C. 64, Box 240, Rimrock, AZ 86335; (520) 567-4501.

Permit: None.

The hike: Drive east out of Camp Verde on the General Crook Trail, Forest Highway 9, to Forest Road 618. Turn left onto Forest Road 618 and drive four miles to Forest Road 214. Turn right onto Forest Road 214 and go 5.6 miles to FR 214A. Unless you have a high clearance vehicle, park here. Otherwise continue 1.2 miles to the trailhead.

The trail descends steeply into the West Clear Creek Canyon then follows the creek downstream about six miles. Several stream crossings are necessary and may be difficult during periods of high water such as the spring runoff or after a heavy thunder shower.

As you near Bull Pen Ranch, the trail turns east away from the creek to avoid the private land. About .5 mile after leaving t he creek, the Blodgett Basin Trail is encountered. This trail climbs about 1500 vertical feet back to the canyon rim and Forest Road 214. Follow FR 214 back to FR 214A and your vehicle.—*Coconino National Forest.*

HIKE 10 *WALKER BASIN TRAIL*

General description: A little used loop trail in the West Clear Creek Wilderness Area.

General location: About nine miles east of Camp Verde.

Maps: Walker Mtn. 7.5-minute, Buckhorn Mtn. 7.5-minute USGS quads; Coconino National Forest map.

Difficulty: Moderate.

Length: About twelve miles round trip.

Elevation: 5,780 to 3,700 feet.

Special attractions: Panoramic views of the Verde Valley and Red Rock Country around Sedona.
Water availability: None.
Best season: Spring and fall.
For more information: Beaver Creek Ranger Station; H.C. 64, Box 240, Rimrock, AZ 86335; (520) 567-4501.
Permit: None.
Wilderness status: None.

The hike: A car shuttle can make this a pleasant one-way dayhike. Drive one vehicle from the Sedona Interchange on In Interstate 17 east on Forest Road 618. About five miles from I-17, look for the marked trailhead on the left side of the road.

The other end of the trail is reached by driving another three miles further on Forest Road 618 to 214. Turn left onto 214 an d go seven miles to the trailhead on the left side of the road.

If you begin this hike at the first trailhead, you gain most of the trail's elevation in the first three miles as it threads along the crest of a ridge. You are treated to great views of the Verde Valley and the Red Rock Country. The trail tops out on the Mogollon Rim and passes between the twin peaks of Walker Mountain before continuing toward Forest Road 214. Stock tanks are the only water sources in this dry country. Carry your own drinking water.—*Coconino National Forest*

HIKE 11 *TOWEL CREEK TRAIL*

General description: An overnight backpack to a remote section of the Verde River.
General location: About 18 miles east of Camp Verde.
Maps: Hackberry Mtn. 7.5-minute, Horner Mtn. 7.5-minute USGS quads; Coconino National Forest map.
Difficulty: Moderate.
Length: Seven miles one way.
Elevation: 4150 to 2800 feet.
Special attractions: Solitude, traces of prehistoric Indians, the Verde River.
Water availability: Towel Spring is unreliable and Verde River.
Best season: Spring, fall, winter.
For more information: Beaver Creek Ranger Station, H.C. 64, Box 240, Rimrock, AZ 86335; (520) 567-4501.
Permit: None.

The hike: Take the General Crook Trail, Forest Highway 9, east out of Camp Verde about seven miles to Forest Road 708 . Turn right onto FR 708 and continue for approximately nine miles to the signed trailhead. The trail climbs slightly to Towel Tank offering fine views of the Mogollon Rim, Fossil Creek Canyon, and Deadman Mesa. On the far south horizon lie the high peaks of the Mazatzal Mountains.

From Towel Tank, the trail follows Towel Creek on its gradual 1,600-foot drop down to the Verde River. The short side-trail to Towel Spring is interesting. The main trail crosses to the north side of Towel Creek downstream of the spring and becomes indistinct for the next .5 mile before it crosses back to the south side of the creek. Look for rock cairns that mark the trail or follow the creek bottom until the trail crossing. Once back on the south side, the trail becomes easier to follow.

An elf owl, north America's smallest owl, was seen near the Verde River one warm, early summer evening. Many other birds nest along the Verde and in the trees growing along Towel Creek.—*Stewart Aitchison.*

HIKE 12 *FOSSIL SPRINGS TRAIL*

General description: A round-trip day hike into the Fossil Springs Wilderness Area.
General location: About six miles west of Strawberry.
Maps: Strawberry 7.5-minute USGS quad; Coconino National Forest map.
Difficulty: Moderate.
Length: About 2.5 miles one way.
Elevation: 5,800 to 4,300 feet.
Special attractions: A lush riparian habitat supported by springs issuing over a million gallons of water an hour.
Water availability: The spring water is permanent but should be purified before drinking.
Best season: Spring and fall.
For more information: Beaver Creek Ranger District, HC 64 Box 240, Rimrock, AZ 86335; (520) 567-4501.
Permit: None

The hike: The Fossil Springs Wilderness was established in 1984 and encompasses some 11,550 acres of rugged canyons carved into the southern edge of the Colorado Plateau. Elevations range from 4300 feet at the springs to 6800 feet on the Mogollon Rim. The wilderness area is nine miles long and four miles wide.

To reach this particular trailhead, drive from Highway 87 in Strawberry about six miles west on Forest Road 708 to a faint turnoff to the north. On the topographic map, this turnoff is shown leading to a gravel pit. The road only goes about a quarter-mile before coming to the wilderness boundary.

The trail, at this point an old road, begins its descent into the main canyon. In about two miles, you reach the floor of the canyon above the springs. Runoff from rain or melting snow may be flowing along this otherwise dry streambed. Following the t rail about one-half mile downstream brings you to the springs where over a million gallons of heavily mineralized, 72 degree temperature water gush out of the ground per hour.

The springs were first discovered by non-Native Americans in the 1880s. The permanent flow allows for the survival of over 30 species of trees and shrubs which in turn provide habitat for over 100 kinds of birds. The stream is home to roundtail chub and possibly the endangered Gila topminnow. The rare black hawk can occasionally be seen in the area.

Other wildlife includes mule deer, white-tailed deer, black bear, mountain lion, javelina, fox, coyote, badger, skunks, ring-tailed cats, rock squirrels, and the Arizona gray squirrel.

The name of the springs refers to the 350 million year old fossiliferous marine limestones exposed. In 1916 a dam and flume were built downstream to divert water to spin turbines located at the Irving Power Plant on the Verde River. The dam, flume, and power plant are still in operation to supply a part of Arizona's electricity needs. Please do not disturb these facilities. The road (closed to public vehicles) leading into the dam from Forest Road 708 offers a less vertical but longer route to the springs.

Calf Pen and Sandrock canyons in the upper, more remote section of the wilderness offer great opportunities for longer trips. An old mail trail drops off the Mogollon Rim from the north and junctions with Fossil Creek approximately 1.5 miles north of the springs. The trailhead is difficult to reach by vehicle and the trail hard to find. For more information contact the Beaver Creek Ranger District.—*Stewart Aitchison* □

HIKE 13 *HIGHLINE TRAIL*

HIKE 13 *HIGHLINE TRAIL*

General description: An extended backpack just below the Mogollon Rim on a National Recreation Trail.

General location: Between Pine and where State Highway 260 ascends the Mogollon Rim.

Maps: Buckhead Mesa 7.5-minute, Kehl Ridge 7.5-minute, Dane Canyon 7.5-minute, Diamond Point 7.5-minute, Promontory Butte 7.5-minute, Woods Canyon 7.5-minute USGS quads; Tonto National Forest map; also the Forest Service has a helpful sketch m map done by Peggy Newman.

Difficulty: Easy to moderate.

Length: Fifty-one miles.

Elevation: 5,400 to 6,800 feet.

Special attractions: Splendid vistas; trout fishing.

Water availability: A number of creeks cross the trail; check with Forest Service for current reliability.

Best season: Although the best times are spring and fall, this trail is usually hikeable all year.

For more information: Payson Ranger District, P.O. Box 100, Payson, AZ 85541; (520) 474-7900.

Permit: None.

Wilderness status: None.

Tunnel and ruins on the Tunnel Trail in the Coconino National Forest. Stewart Aitchison.

The hike: This highly scenic trail travels for fifty-one miles just under the Mogollon Rim in central Arizona. Over fifteen side trails allow you to plan a variety of shorter trips. The trail is well-maintained and easy to follow, although intersections with other trails may cause confusion. Be sure to always check your map.

The west trailhead for the Highline Trail is located about 2.5 miles south of Pine on State Highway 87 and is signed. The east trailhead is on State Highway 260 not quite four miles from the top of the Mogollon Rim. Allow at least five days for traversing the entire route. Parts of the area the trail passes through were burned in the 1990 Dude fire.—*Tonto National Forest*

HIKE 14 *TUNNEL TRAIL*

HIKE 14 *TUNNEL TRAIL*

General description: A short dayhike off the Mogollon Rim.
General location: About fifteen miles north-northeast of Payson.
Maps: Dane Canyon 7.5-minute, Kehl Ridge 7.5-minute USGS quads; Tonto National Forest map.
Difficulty: Easy.
Length: About one mile roundtrip.
Elevation: 7,264 to 6,800 feet.
Special attractions: Sight of abandoned, partially completed railroad tunnel through the Mogollon Rim.
Water availability: None.
Best season: Spring through fall.
For more information: Payson Ranger District, P.O. Box 100, Payson, AZ 85541; (520) 474-7900.
Permit: None.
Wilderness status: None.

The hike: To connect Flagstaff and the Union Pacific Railroad with the mineral district of Morenci, a trans-Mogollon Rim rail line was proposed in 1883. Several years passed before financing became available to allow track to be laid. Thirty-five miles of track heading southeast out of Flagstaff were completed, and a tunnel was started through the Rim. But before the 3,100-foot tunnel was finished, the Arizona Mineral Belt Railroad went bankrupt.

To reach this trail, turn onto the Rim Road, Forest Road 300, from State Highway 87 about thirteen miles north of Strawberry. About fourteen miles in, you will come to an Historical marker for the Battle of Big Dry Wash on the north side of the road. Park here.

To the south, toward the Mogollon Rim is a sign marking the Colonel Devin Trail 290. Start down this trail. In about .5 mile is a signed turnoff to the left for the Tunnel Trail. This trails winds upward a short distance and ends at the uncompleted railroad tunnel and the ruins of a building.—*Stewart Aitchison*

HIKE 15 *HORTON CREEK TRAIL*

General description: Day-hike along a trout stream.
General location: About fifteen miles northeast of Payson.
Maps: Promontory Butte 7.5-minute USGS quad; Tonto National Forest map.
Difficulty: Easy.
Length: About 3.5 miles one way.
Elevation: 5,500 to 6,600 feet.
Special attractions: Trout fishing.
Water availability: Good water at Horton Spring at trail's end.
Best season: All year.

NORTH

Horton
Spring

X
6600'

Horton Creek

Hortoin Creek Trail

Highline
Trail

6600' X

Horton
Campground
X
5500'

Tonto Creek

Derrick Trail

289

Tonto Creek
Campground
X
5400'

Kohls
Ranch

260

One Mile

For more information: Payson Ranger District, P.O. Box 100, Payson, AZ 85541; (520) 474-7900.
Permit: None.
Wilderness status: None.

The hike: Follow State Highway 260 fifteen miles east from Payson to Kohl's Ranch area. Turn north on Tonto Creek Road d 289. Travel one mile to the Horton (Upper Tonto) Campground. Park below entrance gate to campground but do not block road.

The trail begins about 150 feet up the campground road and follows an abandoned logging road which parallels Horton Creek . The trail is within sight of the creek for the first 1.2 miles and within 300 yards the rest of the way. The trail ends near the large, beautiful Horton Spring which gushes out the side of the mountain.

For a longer loop hike, you may continue from Horton Spring along the Highline Trail (see Hike 13) south to the Derrick Trail which leads back to the Upper Tonto Campground.

If you plan to camp in the Horton Spring or Creek vicinity, please stay at least 200 feet from the water.—*Tonto National Forest.*

HIKE 16 *PINE CANYON CREEK*

General description: A day hike or longer up or down the Mogollon Rim.
General location: Near Pine.
Maps: Buckhead Mesa 7.5-minute, Pine 7.5-minute USGS quad; Tonto National Forest map.
Difficulty: Moderate to Difficult.
Length: Eight miles one way.
Elevation: 5,600 to 7,200 feet.
Special attractions: A relatively cool, forested hike which is delightful during the summer.
Water availability: Dripping Springs, Parsnip Springs, and the 1.5 miles that the trail runs along Pine Creek.
Best season: Spring through fall.
For more information: Payson Ranger District, P.O. Box 100, Payson, AZ 85541; (520) 474-7900.
Permit: None.
Wilderness status: None.

The hike: Approximately 2.5 miles south of Pine on State Highway 87 is the signed Highline trailhead. Hike about 450 feet on the Highline trail to reach the Pine Canyon trailhead.

The Pine Canyon Trail offers a variety of sights along its eight miles. The hiker will get several distant views of Pine Canyon on, be treated to rich green fern undergrowth as the trail follows Pine Creek, and get some birds eye views of Pine Canyon as the trail makes its way up to the rim.

The hiker faces a steep climb at the end of the first mile and again at mile six when the trail begins to ascend the Mogollon Rim in a series of switchbacks.

The trail ends on top of the rim on State Highway 87 about two miles north of the Camp Verde turnoff (the General Crook Highway).

A vehicle at each end can make this just a day hike. Obviously the opposite direction which is mostly downhill is the easiest.—*Tonto National Forest* □

HIKE 16 *PINE CANYON CREEK*

NORTH

One Mile

7800' X

One Mile

300

Lookout
Tower

Rim Road

See
Canyon

Rim

Nappa
Spring

See
Spring

Mogollon

Herman
Spring

X 6200'

P

Highline
Trail

Christopher Creek

284

NORTH

260

HIKE 17 *SEE CANYON*

General description: A dayhike up the Mogollon Rim.
General location: About twenty-one miles northeast of Payson.
Maps: Promontory Butte 7.5-minute USGS quad; Tonto National Forest map.
Difficulty: Moderate to difficult.
Length: 3.5 miles one way.
Elevation: 6,200 to 7,800 feet.
Special attractions: Great views off the Mogollon Rim.
Water availability: Christopher Creek is perennial.
Best season: Spring through fall.
For more information: Payson Ranger District, P.O. Box 100, Payson, AZ 85541; (520) 474-7900.
Permit: None.
Wilderness status: None.

The hike: Follow State Highway 260 about twenty-one miles east of Payson and then turn left onto Forest Road 284 just across from a gas station. Follow FR 284 about 1.5 miles and watch for a hiker's sign to the right.

You start this hike by crossing Christopher Creek on the Highline Trail. About 850 feet from the trailhead, you will come to the junction with the See Canyon Trail.

The See Canyon Trail is short but challenging. The first two miles follow Christopher Creek but then the final 1.5 miles climbs steeply to the Mogollon Rim. The trail continues a short distance to the Rim Road, Forest Road 300. Fall is a particularly fine time to hike this trail and to enjoy the autumn colors.—*Tonto National Forest.*

HIKE 18 *OVERLAND TRAIL*

General description: An historically important north-central Arizona trail, parts of which are suitable for hiking.
General location: Flagstaff to Prescott.
Maps: Garland Prairie 7.5-minute, Davenport Hill 7.5-minute, Williams South 7.5-minute USGS quads; Kaibab National Forests (south) map.
Difficulty: Easy to moderate.
Length: Total length approximately eighty-five miles; hike described about nine miles one way.
Elevation: 6,700 to 7,200 feet.
Special attractions: Historical trail.
Water availability: Unreliable stock tanks and springs.
Best season: Late spring through fall.
For more information: Kaibab National Forest, 800 S. 6th St., Williams, AZ 86046; (520) 635-8200; ask for a copy of: *The Overland Road: An Important Historic Arizona Trail on the Kaibab National Forest* by James W. Byrkit.

NORTH

One Mile

173 Barney
Knoll
Lockett
Spring
X
7200'

Hyde
Hill
139
X 6811'
Big
Spring

109

56
13
Dow
Springs 6700'
X
Pomeroy
Tanks
LO
Springs

Permit: None.
Wilderness status: None.

The hike: This trail probably dates back to prehistoric times when it was used by indigenous people including the Hopi. The discovery of gold in the headwaters of the Hassayampa River in 1863 led to the U.S. Army sending Captain Nathaniel Pishon and twenty-five soldiers to establish a post near the mines.

The army's route, from Antelope Spring (now Flagstaff) to what would eventually become Fort Whipple and later Prescott, became known as The Overland Road. This major route served travelers until 1882.

Parts of the original route between Lockwood Spring and Hell Canyon are still used today. Kaibab Forest Roads 354 and 57 lie almost on top of the old road. Forest Road 173 (the Perkinsville Road) follows the Overland Road in several places.

One interesting section to hike is from Dow Springs to Lockwood (Lockett) Spring, a distance of about nine miles one way. From Williams drive south on Forest Road 173, the Perkinsville Road, about eleven miles. Turn left onto Forest Road 139. Drive about nine miles and FR 173 crosses FR 109 and becomes FR 13. Follow FR 13 about three miles where it intersects with FR 56. Turn right on FR 56 and go about .3 mile. Dow Springs feeds into one of the upper drainages to Sycamore Canyon.

The Overland Trail heads basically west to Pomeroy Tanks then to Big Spring, and finally to Lockwood or Lockett Spring. The trail is marked every quarter-mile with brass capped pipes set in the ground. Line-of-sight piled rock cairns serve as markers in between the pipes. By leaving a vehicle at Lockwood Spring, which is near the intersection of FR 173 and FR 139, you can hike this as a one-way day trip. Old wagon wheel ruts are sometimes visible especially around the Pomeroy Tanks area.—*Kaibab National Forest* ☐

Laws Spring along the Beale Road in the Kaibab National Forest. Stewart Aitchison.

HIKE 19 *BEALE ROAD*

General description: A short day-hike along part of an historical route.
General location: About fourteen miles northeast of Williams.
Maps: Squaw Mountain 7.5-minute USGS quad; Kaibab National Forest (south) map.
Difficulty: Easy
Length: One mile one way.
Elevation: 6,800 feet.
Special attractions: Historical inscriptions.
Water availability: Natural rock tank but water is of questionable quality.
Best season: Spring through fall.
For more information: Chalendar Ranger District, 501 W. Bill Williams Ave., Williams, AZ 86046; (520) 635-2676.
Permit: None.
Wilderness status: None.

The hike: The Beale Wagon Road was one of the three major immigrant routes to California prior to the Civil War and brought large numbers of people through northern Arizona. The route was surveyed and constructed between 1857 and 1859 by Lieutenant Edward F. Beale, who commanded the Army's experimental Camel Corps in Arizona. The road roughly followed an earlier route used for centuries by indigenous Native Americans. The Beale Road was a precursor to the 1882 transcontinental Atlantic and Pacific Railroad (later to become the Santa Fe) and Highway Route 66, which has now been replaced by Interstate 40.

Until the railroad arrived, the Beale road was the most important road in Arizona. It continued to be used extensively until the 1940s, and many Forest Service roads presently follow the Beale Road.

The Kaibab National Forest contains the most varied and scenic portion of the entire route from Albuquerque, New Mexico, to the Colorado River, including the highest elevation of the road, and according to Beale, some of the grandest views.

About twenty-three miles of the road is located on the Kaibab National Forest and much of it can be seen today. Ask at any Kaibab Ranger Station for more route information. Although the Beale Road was a major artery of westward travel and built according to the standards of the time, it was never much more than a dirt track. Today it appears as a cleared area or slight depression about ten feet wide with rocks hand-piled to either side. It is occasionally defined by trees of the same size growing on the edges, with smaller trees in the roadbed, or by wheel ruts in open ground.

One section of special interest to hikers is to first drive north on Forest Road 74 from the Pitman Valley exit on Interstate 40 east of Williams. FR 74 intersects with FR 141. Turn right to FR 730. Go north on FR 730 until you hit FR 115 at Boulin Tank. Follow FR 115 about two miles looking for a faint road coming in on your right, shown as FR 2033 on the Kaibab National Forest map but not signed. At this juncture, you may be able to find a short, brass-capped pipe which indicates the Beale Road. Park here.

The original Beale Road heads northwesterly, roughly paralleling FR 2030. Look for rock cairns and other brass-capped pipes marking the route. In about a mile, veer a little to the north to drop into a shallow drainage to find Laws Spring. This spring was an import ant water source to early travelers. There are several historic inscriptions scratched into the basalt rocks around the spring.

Return to your vehicle by either retracing your steps or, from the spring, walk northeasterly and intersect FR 2030 and follow it back to FR 115.— *Stewart Aitchison & Kaibab National Forest*

HIKE 20 *JOHNSON CANYON*

General description: A short day-hike along an historic route.
General location: About fifteen miles west of Williams.
Maps: Ash Fork 7.5-minute, McLellan Reservoir 7.5-minute, Hearst Mountain 7.5-minute USGS quads; Kaibab National (south) Forest map.
Difficulty: Easy.
Length: 2.5 miles one way.
Elevation: 5932 to 6300 feet.
Special attractions: The only tunnel on the original Atlantic and Pacific Transcontinental Railroad.
Water availability: None.
Best season: Spring through fall.
For more information: Williams Ranger District, Rt. 1, Box 142, Williams, AZ 86046; (520) 635-2633.
Permit: None.
Wilderness status: None.

The hike: Take Interstate 40 west from Williams for about twelve miles and exit at the Welch Interchange. Take Forest Road six north for about two miles. On the left, you will see Johnson Crater, a large sinkhole or collapsed cave. Just past Johnson Crater is a road junction called Welch Siding. Park here.

The concrete pads at Welch Siding are the remains of the railroad siding house used in the 1940s and 1950s. To the right, you will se a narrow roadbed leading into Johnson Canyon. This is what remains of the old abandoned railroad bed. The sheer walls and curves of the four-mile long canyon were an engineering challenge to builders of the 1881-1882 Atlantic and Pacific Railroad. Two bridges and a tunnel were needed to navigate the canyon. The bridges have long since been replaced by earth embankments, but Johnson Tunnel still exists. It was the only tunnel located along the entire span of the transcontinental railroad. A pleasant 2.5 mile walk down the railroad bed brings you to the tunnel, which is still privately owned by the Santa Fe Railroad.—*Kaibab National Forest.*

HIKE 21 *BEAVER DAM MOUNTAINS*

General description: Short round-trip day hike into the Beaver Dam Mountains Wilderness Area.
General location: Eight miles northeast of Littlefield.
Maps: Mountain Sheep Spring 7.5-minute USGS quad; BLM Paiute Primitive Area map.
Difficulty: Easy (cross-country).
Length: As much as three miles one way.
Elevation: 2,700 to 2,900 feet.
Special attractions: Joshua trees, desert tortoises, solitude.
Water availability: None.

Best season: Spring and fall.
For more information: Bureau of Land Management, Arizona Strip District Office, 345 E. Riverside Dr., St. George, UT 84770; (801) 628-4491.
Permit: None.

The hike: Exit at the Virgin River Canyon Recreation Site Exit and follow the primitive dirt road that heads north. There are no established trails in the Beaver Dam Mountains Wilderness Area that straddles this dirt access road. Simply stop where you wish and enjoy a stroll through the beautiful Joshua tree forest. A short walk here is a great introduction to the unique and occasionally bizarre flora and fauna of the Mojave and Great Basin deserts. Adventurous hikers can gain access to the Beaver Dam range itself by traveling cross-country up any of the boulder-strewn drainages.

The handsome collared lizard is frequently seen basking on boulders in Arizona's wildlands. Male lizards found in the Colorado Plateau area of northern Arizona are usually a striking blue-green color, while those found in the low deserts of southern and western Arizona are often brown. Males, such as this one, are usually brighter than females. When alarmed, the collared lizard may flee by running on only its hind legs. Stewart Aitchison

Joshua trees are related to yuccas and therefore are members of the lily family. These trees are typical of the Mojave Desert, but here Mojave Desert species are intermingled with Great Basin species.

Joshua trees do not bloom every yea the interval between blooms is determined by rainfall and temperature. The species' name was given by Mormons who thought the trees seemed to be lifting their "arms" in supplication as did the Biblical Joshua. Paiutes wove the small red roots of Joshua trees into baskets to make designs.

If you are lucky, you may see the endangered desert tortoise. You will certainly encounter Gambel's quail. The name of these mountains comes from the beaver lodges that were to be found along the main drainage on the western side of the range, near present-day Littlefield.—*Stewart Aitchison*

HIKE 22 *MOUNT BANGS*

General description: Long round-trip overnighter to the highest point in the Paiute Wilderness Area.
General location: Eight miles southeast of Littlefield.
Maps: Mountain Sheep Spring 7.5-minute USGS quad, and Mt. Bangs 7.5-minute USGS quad.
Difficulty: Difficult (mostly cross-country).
Length: About twelve miles one way.
Elevation: 2,700 to 8,012 feet.
Special attractions: Fantastic views of three states from the summit.

Water availability: None until Atkin Spring.
Best season: Spring and fall.
For more information: Bureau of Land Management, Arizona Strip District Office, 390N 3050E, St. George, UT 8 4770; (801) 673-3545.
Permit: None.

The hike: To find the trailhead, drive about twenty miles southwest of St. George, Utah on Interstate 15. Exit at the Virgin River Canyon Recreation Site and Campground. On the south side of the campground, ford the Virgin River. Then walk about 1.5 miles downstream to the mouth of Sullivan Canyon. The route up the canyon is rough and rocky now, although a trail is planned for the future. Near the head of Sullivan Canyon, climb west up through the natural break, West Fork Gate to Atkin Spring. A trail from the spring leads ads southwesterly toward Mount Bangs. About a mile before reaching the summit, the trail divides. One branch goes north as the Virgin Ridge Trail; a second goes south to what is called the South Trailhead in Cottonwood Wash; and a third trail, which you follow, goes toward Mount Bangs. In another mile, the trail ends on the ridge that runs up to the summit of Mount Bangs, the goal and turnaround point of this hike.

Along the way you may encounter bighorn sheep. They were indigenous here at one time, but had disappeared from the range by the 1930s. In 1981 bighorns from the Kingman area were transplanted to this mountain range.

The Virgin Mountains stand between two great geologic provinces, the Basin and Range region to the west and the Colorado Plateau to the east. The route begins in a mix of Great Basin and Mohave desert plants such as Joshua trees and sagebrush, then moves up through pinyon-juniper woodland to an island of ponderosa pine. Mount Bangs, which was named by the eminent geologist Clarence Dutton after his clerk James E. Bangs, supports a small stand of Douglas fir and white fir.—*Stewart Aitchison*

HIKE 23 *MOUNT LOGAN*

General description: Short, round-trip day hike in the Mount Logan Wilderness Area.
General location: Sixty-five miles south of St. George, Utah and fifty-five miles southwest of Fredonia.
Maps: Mt. Logan 7.5-minute, Mt. Trumbull NW 7.5-minute USGS quads.
Difficulty: Easy (cross-country).
Length: About .5 miles one way.
Elevation: 7,600 to 7,866 feet.
Special attractions: Merriam's turkeys.
Water availability: None.
Best season: Spring through fall.
For more information: Bureau of Land Management, Arizona Strip District Office, 345 E. Riverside Dr., St. George, UT 84770; (801) 628-4491.
Permit: None.

The hike: Mount Logan can be reached via the Toroweap Road that exits Arizona 389, eight miles west of Fredonia. After about forty-six miles of dirt road, you will come to a major fork in the road. Take the right branch heading west toward Mount Trumbull. Just before the Nixon Spring reservoir and corral, turn left (south) and drive about four miles to a major or fork. The right fork continues to near the top of Mount Logan.

There is a faint trail from the end of the road to the summit and a spectacular view into the eroded west side of the mountain called Hells Hole. In 1858, Lt. Joseph Christmas Ives called this volcanic range the North Side Mountains, a reference to the fact that these mountains are on the north side of the Grand Canyon. Fourteen years later, Maj. John Wesley Powell christened this peak after U.S. Senator John Logan.

Like Mounts Trumbull and Emma, Mount Logan is an extinct volcano. This section of the Arizona Strip Country was the scene of tremendous volcanic activity during the late Cenozoic time. Lava flows filled entire canyons and even spilled into the Grand Canyon, damming the Colorado River.—*Stewart Aitchison* □

HIKE 24 *MOUNT TRUMBULL*

HIKE 24 *MOUNT TRUMBULL*

General description: A short round-trip day hike on an ancient volcano in the Mount Trumbull Wilderness Area.

General location: Eighty miles south of St. George, Utah and 55 miles southwest of Fredonia.

Maps: Mount Trumbull NW 7.5-minute USGS quad.

Difficulty: Easy.

Length: About 3.0 miles one way.

Elevation: 6,400 to 8,028 feet.

Special attractions: Historic sites and the unique Kaibab squirrel.

Water availability: Water pump near the trailhead.

Best season: Spring through fall.

For more information: Bureau of Land Management, Arizona Strip District Office, 345 E. Riverside Dr., St. George, UT 84770; (801) 628-4491.

Permit: None.

The hike: Mount Trumbull is accessible via the Toroweap Road that branches off of Arizona 389, eight miles west of Fredonia. After about forty-six miles of dirt road, you will come to a major fork in the road. Take the right branch heading west toward Mount Trumbull.

In about six miles you will come to Nixon Rnager Station, the site of a steam-powered sawmill built by Mormons in 1870. An interpretive sign marks the location. Here, Mormons cut ponderosa timbers for the construction of the St. George Temple. The timbers were hauled by oxen over eighty miles to St. George. The wagon ruts are still visible today.

At the trailhead is a register and a parking lot. A good trail takes you to the summit for a grand view of the Arizona Strip Country.

Kaibab squirrels, a strikingly handsome beast endemic to the North Rim of the Grand Canyon, were introduced on Mount Trumbull in the 1970s. These tassel-eared fellows eat ponderosa pine seeds and certain fungi associated with the pines.

Mount Trumbull was named after U.S. Senator Lyman Trumbull by Major John Wesley Powell during his exploration of the Arizona Strip in 1871-1872.

Except during the deer hunting season, the hiker is unlikely to encounter anyone in this area.—*Stewart Aitchison.*

HIKE 25 *SURPRISE CANYON*

General description: A round-trip day hike or backpack into a remote part of the Grand Canyon.

General location: About fifty miles northeast of Kingman.

Maps: Spencer Canyon 7.5-minute, Devils Slide Rapid 7.5- minute, Amos Point 7.5-minute, Mount Dellenbaugh 7.5-minute, Whitmore Point SW 7.5-minute USGS quads.
Difficulty: Moderate to difficult (cross-country).
Length: Fourteen miles or more one way.
Elevation: 1,250 to 3,500 feet or more.
Special attractions: Remoteness, incredible geology.
Water availability: A stream flows intermittently along the canyon floor.
Best season: Fall through spring.
For more information: Grand Canyon National Park, P.O. Box 129, Grand Canyon, AZ 86023; (520) 638-7888.
Permit: Required from National Park Service for overnight camping.
Wilderness status: Administratively endorsed wilderness.

The hike: This trip is unique in that it requires a boat to reach the trailhead. If you have launched your boat from Pierce Ferry on Lake Mead, you will need to cruise about thirty-two miles upstream to reach the mouth of Surprise Canyon.

One of the canyon's surprises is the sand bar that sometimes forms at the canyon's mouth. This bar can prevent your boat from entering the canyon if the lake level is down.

The canyon may have received its name from the large area that drains into such an inconspicuous slot through the granite at the river. The creek is also exceptional in that it is not necessary to carry water for the long (about fourteen miles) trailless hike up to the junction with Twin Springs Canyon. Water runs on the surface and then disappears, but you are never more than forty-five minutes from where the water reappears.

Kanab Creek is the major north-side drainage to the Grand Canyon and has numerous side-canyons which provide endless possibilities for exploration. Bruce Grubbs

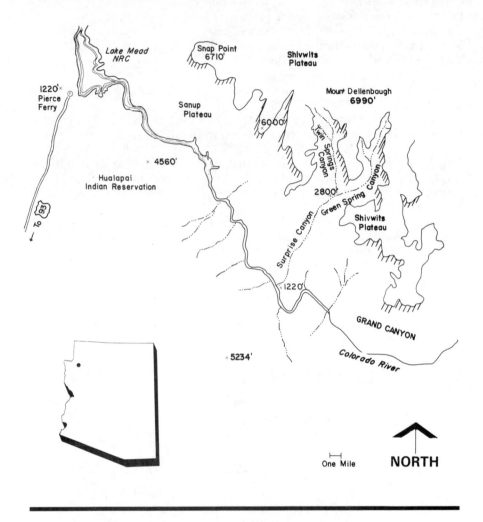

One Mile

NORTH

The walking is slow because of flood-scattered boulders. Some wading may be necessary. Take special care of the footing—many hikers have suffered nasty falls here.

Surprise Canyon has several fine overhangs that will shelter you on a wet night, especially near the top of the Tapeats Sandstone and in the Redwall Limestone near the junction with Twin Springs Canyon.

Surprise Canyon has so many intriguing features that it has become a favorite haunt of mine. For instance, there is a natural bridge on the east side about .3 mile up the bed from the west border of the Amos Point quad. From a little distance, this place looks like a simple overhang and there is no big drainage in it.

The many side canyons invite exploration. Some have fantastic narrows cut into the Redwall Limestone. About a mile up Twin Springs Canyon, you reach the narrowest and deepest Redwall gorge I have ever seen. Others, such as the Green Spring Arm, contain pools that require swimming.

This is a great place for the exploratory hiker.—*Harvey Butchart*

Editors' note: Harvey Butchart is *the* authority on hiking in the Grand Canyon area. This trail description has been paraphrased from his extensive hiking notes that cover over forty years of Grand Canyon exploration.

HIKE 26 *HACK CANYON*

General description: A round-trip day hike in the Kanab Creek Wilderness Area.
General location: Thirty-five miles south of Fredonia, off the Mount Trumbull—Toroweap Road.
Maps: Grama Draw 7.5-minute USGS quad.
Difficulty: Moderate.
Length: About two miles one way.
Elevation: 5,100 to 3,900 feet.
Special attractions: Access to spectacular Kanab Canyon and its side canyons.
Water: Willow Spring.
Best season: Spring and fall.
For more information: Bureau of Land Management, Arizona Strip District Office, 345 E. Riverside Dr., St. George, UT 84770; (801) 628-4491.
Permit: None unless camping within Grand Canyon National Park.

The hike: From Fredonia, drive west on Arizona 389 about eight miles to the Toroweap Road. Drive south about thirty miles on this graded dirt road. Two miles before crossing the low ridge at CCC Trail Reservoir (the Heaton Knolls map will be useful), turn south and follow the best road about six miles to the rim of Hack Canyon. The road now turns east and follows the rim. Watch for a small corral out on the very rim of the canyon about a mile east of the point where the road met the rim. The Hack Canyon Trail starts from this corral.

From the corral, the trail descends west a short distance, then switchbacks to the east below the rim cliffs. It works its way through a break in the buff-colored Coconino Sandstone cliff, then drops onto a broad talus fan and descends directly to the bed of Hack Canyon. A few hundred yards upstream is Willow Spring on the south bank. The spring seems to be reliable but should be purified. From the spring, it is an easy walk downstream to Kanab Canyon, the turnaround point for this hike but an excellent starting point for your own exploratory hikes.

The Hack Trail is a good access route for extended trips in the Kanab Canyon-Jumpup Canyon area. You enter Grand Canyon National Park at Jumpup Canyon, and a permit is required for camping within the park. The Hack Trail was probably built by cattle ranchers for access to Willow Spring, which is a valuable source of water on the dry Arizona Strip.

HIKE 26 *HACK CANYON*

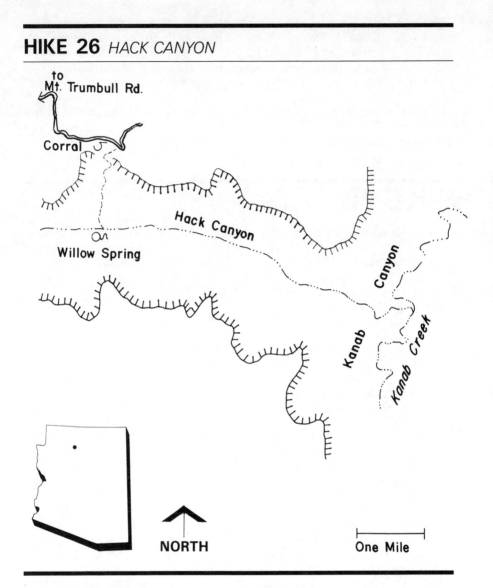

The area is part of a BLM wilderness area established in 1984. A few miles upstream of Willow Spring, an old uranium mine has been reopened with possible impacts on the remote character of the Arizona Strip. For example, the miners would like to see the Toroweap Road paved to improve all-weather access to the mine area.—*Bruce Grubbs* □

HIKE 27 *JUMPUP CANYON*

General description: A round-trip two- or three-day backpack in Kanab Creek Wilderness Area.

General location: Twenty-five miles south of Fredonia.

Maps: Jumpup Point 7.5-minute, Fishtail 7.5-minute, Kanab Point 7.5-minute USGS quads; Kaibab National Forest North map.

Difficulty: Moderate to difficult (cross-country).

Length: About ten miles one way to Kanab Canyon.

Elevation: 5,600 to 2,600 feet.

Special attractions: Scenic and remote access to Kanab Creek in western Grand Canyon.

Water: Lower Jumpup Spring, near Kanab Creek.

Best season: Spring and fall.

For more information: North Kaibab Ranger District, P.O. Box 248, Fredonia, AZ 86022; (520) 643-7395.

Permit: Required downstream of confluence of Jumpup and Kanab creeks within Grand Canyon National Park.

The hike: Jumpup Canyon is one of the many scenic arms of Kanab Creek. Much of this area has been recently added to Gr and Canyon National Park. Additional areas in Jumpup and upper Kanab Canyons have been protected as wilderness administered by the Forest Service and Bureau of Land Management.

Turn off U.S. 89A about twenty-five miles east of Fredonia and go south on Forest Road 422A. About twelve miles south of the highway, turn west(right) on Forest Road 423 and follow this road to its end in Jumpup Canyon. There are many forks, so follow the road signs carefully. This road is normally passable to high-clearance vehicles except in winter or early spring.

An old cabin marks the end of the road, and the Jumpup Trail starts from the east side of the old corral and immediately starts down the canyon. After about a mile the trail reaches the canyon floor, and a sign points out Jumpup Spring. This spring is not reliable.

Although the Forest Service map shows Trail 41 continuing down Jumpup Canyon, it no longer exists for practical purposes. However, it is easy walking down the dry gravel streambed about four miles to Lower Jumpup Spring, which is reliable.

Below Lower Jumpup Spring, the stream bed normally has running water, and the walking gets somewhat rougher. In the red Supai Sandstone formation, you come to a high waterfall, bypassing it on the southeast. You will probably need to lower your packs on a rope. About two miles below Lower Jumpup Spring, you come to Sowats Canyon on the left (east). In another mile you pass the entrance to Kwagunt Hollow and in yet another mile, the entrance to Indian Hollow. These are all interesting and beautiful canyons to explore.

From Sowats Canyon, it is about five miles to Kanab Creek. Much of this section is in spectacular narrows cut through the Red wall Limestone. In comparison, Kanab Canyon seems almost spacious. The narrows is usually dry but is subject to dangerous flash flooding and should not be hiked if water is running or there is any danger of rain in the headwaters. About a mile above the junction with Kanab Canyon, a pothole below a dry waterfall on the right usually has water. Kanab Creek has permanent water a couple of miles below Jumpup Creek, and is the turnaround point for a two- or three-day round-trip hike.

South of Jumpup Creek you enter Grand Canyon National Park and a permit is required for overnight camping within the Park. Many more days can be spent exploring the side canyons of Jumpup and Kanab canyons. Jumpup is but an introduction to this fine area.—*Bruce Grubbs* □

HIKE 28 NORTH CANYON

General description: A round-trip day hike into the Saddle Mountain Wilderness Area.
General location: Twenty miles north of the North Rim of the Grand Canyon.
Maps: Dog Point 7.5-minute USGS quad; Kaibab National Forest (north) map.
Difficulty: Moderate.
Length: Six miles or less one way.
Elevation: 7,540 to 8,800 feet.
Special attractions: Apache trout in the small stream.

HIKE 28 NORTH CANYON

Water availability: A small permanent stream.
Best season: Summer and fall.
For more information: North Kaibab Ranger District, P.O. Box 248, Fredonia, AZ 86022; (6520) 643-7395.
Permit: None.

The hike: This hike offers amazing views from the Kaibab Plateau into House Rock Valley and the Marble Canyon area. Hikers may also fish for the rare Apache trout, which is endemic to the White Mountains of east-central Arizona but has recently been stocked here.

To find the trailhead, go about 1.5 miles south of the Kaibab Lodge and turn left onto Forest Road 611. Follow 611 about four miles to the East Rim Viewpoint.

The trail begins here and switchbacks steeply down into North Canyon, visible below during your descent. If you follow the trail all 6 miles, you pass through a number of different life zones or plant communities from spruce-fir forest down to sagebrush desert. The maples and other deciduous trees along the creek are exceptionally beautiful during the fall.

The trail ends at Forest Road 631.—*Gary Russell*

HIKE 29 *JACOB'S POOLS*

General description: A round-trip day hike following remnants of an old trail into the Paria Canyon-Vermilion Cliffs Wilderness Area.
General location: Twenty miles east of Jacob Lake.
Maps: Emmett Hill 7.5-minute, Emmitt Wash 7.5-minute USGS quads.
Difficulty: Moderate (mostly cross-country).
Length: About three miles one way.
Elevation: 5,200 to 6,800 feet.
Special attractions: Spectacular views of House Rock Valley.
Best season: Fall through spring.
For more information: Bureau of Land Management, Arizona Strip District Office, 345 E. Riverside Dr., St. George, UT 84770; (801) 628-4491.
Permit: None.

The hike: This primitive, unmaintained trail is about twenty miles east of Jacob Lake. Turn off U.S. 89A just west of milepost 557, which is about two hundred yards east of an historical marker. Follow this road past the corral over the hill and down into the area where plastic tubes bring water from the seeps in the clay hills down to the pool.

In places where trails are intermittent or non-existent, human or animal tracks are often the next-best thing. On this hike, for instance, I followed the footprints of three or four people going up the sandy slope toward the break in the rim above. When I was about halfway up the whole slope, I went to the south because I found some cairns in that direction; the tracks I had been observing, however, went more directly up. Before I had gone far enough south to use the man-made trail to the top, I followed deer tracks up through the broken slope consisting of sand and loose rocks. When I was nearing the final arrow ravine through the top cliff, I recognized a well-built retaining wall and realized that I was finally on the right route.

I noticed the "G.M. Wright, 20 April 1894" inscription right away and also quite a few very old pecked-in petroglyphs stained with desert varnish, an iron or manganese oxide deposit. I made it *to the top* in 1 hour, 45 minutes. Before turning around, I also saw other petroglyphs and a wild beehive in a fissure in the cliff right near some of the best rock art.

Descending, I was able to detect and follow more of the old trail. Incidentally, I also saw more recent inscriptions than the one of 1894. Someone had scratched "Spence" on the wall with the date 1941.—*Harvey Butchart* □

Editors note: Harvey Butchart is *the* authority on hiking in the Grand Canyon area. This trail description has been paraphrased from his notes of an exploratory trip to Jacob's Pool.

HIKE 30 *SALIENT POINT*

General description: Very remote round-trip day hike in the Paria Canyon-Vermilion Cliffs Wilderness Area.
General location: West of Marble Canyon.
Maps: One Toe Ridge 7.5-minute, The Big Knoll 7.5-minute USGS quads.
Difficulty: Easy.
Length: About a mile one way.
Elevation: 7,000 to 7,200 feet.
Special attractions: Rare and spectacular view of Marble Canyon.
Water: None.

The Paria River in the Paria-Vermillion Cliffs Wilderness Area. Bruce Grubbs

HIKE 30 *SALIENT POINT*

To House Rock Valley Road

Paria Plateau

Round Valley

Stock Tank

Joes Ranch

Pinnacle Valley

To Jarvas Ranch

White Knolls

Salient
7187

Vermilion Cliffs

Soap Creek

4400

NORTH

One Mile

Best season: April through October.
For more information: Bureau of Land Management, Arizona Strip District Office, 345 E. Riverside Dr., St. George, UT 84770; (801) 628-4491.
Permit: None.

The hike: This long drive and short hike takes you to the rim of the Vermilion Cliffs above Marble Canyon and is well worth the trip for the expansive view. Leave U.S. 89A at House Rock (just before the ascent west onto the Kaibab Plateau), and drive north on a good dirt road about ten miles to another road going east (right) onto the Paria Plateau. This road becomes very sandy a short distance after the junction and four wheel drive is necessary. It will be necessary to use the maps closely to find the remainder of the route.

When the road drops into Pinnacle Valley, go south to a steel stock tank, then east-northeast on the main road to Joes Ranch. About .5 mile west of the ranch, a fork goes south at a stock tank. Stay on this to the end at a stock tank below some white cliffs. The road is shown correctly on the topos except for the turnoff at Joes Ranch.

Walk south onto the mesa and continue cross-country .75 mile to the highest point of the rim, your turnaround point and marked by the "Salient" benchmark. There are places to camp, but you will have to carry water.

The Vermilion Cliffs are formed of Navajo Sandstone, a formation of petrified sand dunes responsible for much of the red rock desert of northern Arizona and southern Utah. The top surface of the sandstone has eroded into deep and loose sand, making the roads in this area difficult or impossible without four-wheel drive. Most of the Paria Plateau north of the Cliffs is covered with pinyon-juniper forest, but ponderosa pines are found in the highest areas. There are many interesting places to explore in the Paria Canyon-Vermilion Cliffs Wilderness Area: famous ones like Paria Canyon and unknown ones like Coyote Buttes.—*Bruce Grubbs*

HIKE 31 *BLUE SPRINGS*

General description: A round-trip day hike or backpack into the remote Little Colorado River Gorge.
General location: Thirty miles northwest of Cameron.
Maps: Blue Spring 7.5-minute, Salt Trail Canyon 7.5-minute USGS quads.
Difficulty: Extremely rugged, borders on climbing.
Length: About 1.5 miles one way.
Elevation: 5,400 to 3,200 feet.

Most of the Blue Springs route is more scramble than hike. This is not a trip for beginning hikers, nor for those who suffer from vertigo. But for the experienced backpacker, Blue Springs and other sections of the Little Colorado River Gorge offer splendid wilderness adventures. Stewart Aitchison

Special attractions: A little-used route into a weird canyon.
Water availability: Blue Springs is permanent but highly mineralized.
Best season: Spring and fall.
For more information: Grand Canyon National Park, P.O. Box 129, Grand Canyon, AZ 86023; (520) 638-7888.

Permit: Technically a permit is required from the Navajo Tribe since this trail is on the reservation; however, since ingress is usually made through Grand Canyon National Park, the park service has issued permits in the past.

Wilderness status: None (Navajo Reservation).

The hike: Finding this trailhead is nearly as challenging as the hike. You can approach it either by starting at Desert View within Grand Canyon National Park or heading north off of Arizona 64. In either case, the idea is to eventually end up due east of Gold Butte. (The first time I tried to find this trail, I ended up in one drainage south of the proper one. We got partway down, but were cliffed out. It is really quite hopeless to describe the route since it varies from season to seas on and year to year. The best advice is to consult the topo map frequently, locate Gold Hill before leaving the pavement, and take the dirt roads that seem to head in that general direction. Eventually you will reach your destination.

Once you are on the rim of the Little Colorado River Gorge due east of Gold Hill, there are rock cairns marking the trailhead . The first couple of switchbacks are surprisingly like a horse trail, but then the trail degenerates into a scramble. Cairns and painted arrows direct you downward. There is at least one spot where most hikers will want to shed their packs and hand them down. A rope for belaying may be wise for one vertical section near the top. In the 1960s, a hiker from Flagstaff fell off this "trail" and broke both her legs, so be forewarned.

Near the end of the trail, as you approach the unmistakable, final "Inner Gorge" formed by the Redwall Limestone, the trail once again appears to be a horse trail. But this good path of only several hundred yards ends at the brink of the final cliff. To reach the river, go upstream a few hundred feet to a break in the cliff. There is a good campsite on the far side of the Little Colorado, which is dry most of the year above the spring and thus no problem to cross. If, however, the river is in flood, think twice about crossing it or your silt-laden body may never be found.

The reward of this epic is, of course, Blue Springs. When the Little Colorado River is not in flood (usually flooding occurs during the spring run-off and then again after heavy summer thundershowers), Blue Springs gushes from the left (west) bank. The water has an incredible azure color due to mineralization, and as it rushes out of the rock, the water actually fizzes because it is so highly charged with carbon dioxide gas.—*Stewart Aitchison.*

HIKE 32 *RED BUTTE*

General description: A round-trip day hike near the Grand Canyon.
General location: Ten miles south of the south rim of Grand Canyon.
Maps: Red Butte 7.5-minute quad; Kaibab National Forest (south) map.
Difficulty: Easy.
Length: One mile one way.
Elevation: 6,000 to 6,700 feet.
Special attractions: Unique view of the Grand Canyon, Coconino Plateau, and San Francisco Peaks.

Water: None.
Best season: April through November.
For more information: Tusayan Ranger District, P.O. Box 3088, Tusayan, AZ 86023; (520) 638-2443.
Permit: None.
Wilderness status: None—in fact, a uranium mine is operating in the area.

The hike: From Flagstaff, drive north on U.S. 180 to Valle (the junction with Arizona 64). This point may also be reached from Williams via Arizona 64. Drive north eleven miles to the Kaibab National Forest boundary and turn east on Forest Road 320. Here a sign describes Red Butte and its unique geology. Drive 1.5 miles east and turn north on Forest Road 340. Drive about .8 mile north and turn east on Forest Road 340A, which ends at the marked trailhead in about .25 mile.

The well-constructed trail winds gradually up the pinyon-juniper forested southwestern slopes of the butte, climbing about seven hundred feet to the summit, which is your turnaround point. If it is manned, the Forest Service fire lookout offers hikers the best view. Be sure to ask the lookout's permission before climbing the single flight of stairs.

Red Butte is one of two surviving remnants of Mesozoic rock formations near the Grand Canyon. The upper walls of the Grand Canyon and the surface of the Coconino Plateau are composed of much older Paleozoic rocks. But only a few dozen miles to the east, these older rocks are buried under many thousands of feet of "middle aged" Mesozoic rocks. These rocks once covered the Grand Canyon area but have been completely eroded away, leaving only the small remnants at Red Butte and Cedar Mountain.—*Bruce Grubbs*

HIKE 33 *RAINBOW BRIDGE TRAIL*

General description: Two- to three-day round-trip backpack trip.
General location: Just across the Utah line, east of Page, Arizona.
Maps: Rainbow Bridge 7.5-minute, Chaiyahi Flat 7.5-minute USGS quads.
Difficulty: Moderate.
Length: Twelve miles one way.
Elevation: 6,300 to 3,700 feet.
Special attractions: Spectacular trail along the flanks of Navajo Mountain to Rainbow Bridge, one of the most beautiful natural bridges in the world.
Water: Cliff Canyon, Rainbow Bridge.
Best season: September-November, April-May.
For more information: Rainbow Bridge National Monument, P.O. Box 1507, Page, AZ 86040; (520) 645-2471.
Permit: Required. Obtain from Navajo Indian Reservation, P.O. Box 9000, Window Rock, AZ 86515; (520) 871-6647.
Wilderness status: None.

The hike: Leave U.S. 160 west of Cow Springs and turn north on Arizona 98. After about 12 miles, turn right (north) on the dirt Navajo Mountain Road. Stay on this road for about 33 miles to a main junction where the right fork goes to Navajo Mountain School. Take the left fork (there may be a sign for Rainbow Bridge Trail or Rainbow Lodge) about 6.5 miles to the road end at the ruins of Rainbow Lodge. There may be signs at the numerous minor forks in this road; it helps to have the Chaiyahi Flat map.

The Rainbow Bridge Trail is the classic approach to Rainbow Bridge Natural

Lake Powell
3700'

Rainbow Bridge
× 3700'
△ Echo Camp

Bridge Canyon

Cliff

Redbud Pass

Spring

Canyon

Navajo Mtn.
10388 ×

Horse Canyon

NORTH

One Mile

Rainbow Lodge
(Ruin)
6300'

To 160

Monument, and was the easiest route before the flooding of Glen Canyon by Lake Powell. Although the trail is only twelve miles long one way, the terrain is rugged enough that many parties take more than two days for the round trip, though it is certainly possible to do the trip in two. Rainbow Bridge is only the crowning glory of the trip. The walk in through enchanted glens of stone with the majestic dome of Navajo Mountain rising above is reward enough in itself.

From the site of Rainbow Lodge (a former commercial lodge and the beginning of guided pack trips to the Bridge), follow an old jeep trail northwest about a hundred yards, after which the trail contours west along the pinyon-juniper covered slope. After less than a mile it crosses First Canyon, the first of several canyon crossings as the trail skirts the rugged slopes of Navajo Mountain. About four miles from the trailhead it reaches a pass at the head of Cliff Canyon, then rapidly descends a steep talus slope to the bed of the canyon.

About two miles farther there is a spring in the bed which offers seasonal water along with a number of possible campsites. After another mile in Cliff Canyon the trail turns north and climbs over Redbud Pass (actually a joint, or crack, in the Navajo Sandstone) to Redbud Creek. The trail then follows Redbud Creek to Bridge Canyon. Hikers round a left turn in the canyon and suddenly the bridge and the end of the hike are visible. Old Echo Camp, used by commercial pack trips for many years before the creation of Lake Powell, offers camping possibilities just before entering the National Monument itself, and serves as the turnaround point of this hike.

Although Glen Canyon Dam sometimes backs water under the bridge (the subject of a long and bitter controversy, finally settled by the U.S. Supreme Court, over artificially flooding a National Monument), the boat dock was fortunately kept out of sight of the bridge. When waterborne tourists are

Although Rainbow Bridge is located in Utah, the described hike begins in Arizona and traverses some of the most fantastic sandstone canyon country anywhere. In the background is snow-covered Navajo Mountain, a volcanic laccolith reaching over 10,000 feet above sea level. Bruce Grubbs

absent, hikers can get a feel for the remoteness of this area before development of the dam and Lake Powell.

As shown on the Navajo Mountain map, another, longer trail skirts the north slopes of Navajo Mountain. This trail is much less used than the Rainbow Lodge Trail, and offers access to the labyrinth of redrock canyons flanking the mountain.—*Bruce Grubbs*

HIKE 34 *KEET SEEL*

General description: An overnight round-trip backpack to Arizona's largest cliff dwelling.
General location: Fifteen miles west of Kayenta.
Maps: Marsh Pass 7.5-minute, Keet Seel Ruin 7.5-minute, Betatakin Ruin 7.5-minute USGS quads.
Difficulty: Easy.
Length: Eight miles one way.
Elevation: 7,000 to 6,300 feet.
Special attractions: Very well preserved Anasazi cliff dwellings, beautiful sandstone canyon, an opportunity to experience the Navajo Reservation.
Water availability: Seasonal water that should be considered polluted by livestock. Carry your own.

The prehistoric Anasazi Indians lived in northern Arizona from about the time of Christ until the fourteenth century. During this 1,300-year span only the last century saw extensive use of cliff houses such as this one, known today as Keet Seel. Earlier Anasazi lived in pit houses, which were partially subterranean huts, or in mud-and-stone pueblos. Stewart Aitchison.

Best season: Trail is only open from Memorial Day through Labor Day.
For more information: Navajo National Monument, HC 71 Box 3, Tonalea, AZ 86044; (520) 672-2366.
Permit: A permit is required from Navajo National Monument; reservations are recommended and can be made up to two months in advance.
Wilderness status: None.

The hike: The ruins, drawings, and artifacts of The Ancient Ones are common across northeastern Arizona. One of the most spectacular Anasazi villages is the 160-room cliff dwelling known as Keet Seel.

Keet Seel is a Navajo phrase meaning "broken pieces of pottery." As you hike up the canyon bottom, potshards litter the sand. From the mid-tenth century to the late thirteenth century, several hundred people occupied Tsegi Canyon and its tributary, Keet Seel, and built several cliff dwellings. Here they grew corn, beans, and squash, tended turkeys, and molded exquisite pottery painted with geometric and animal designs. Then in the late 1200s, the people began to leave. What caused the abandonment—drought, disease, war, or over—population is uncertain.

Even without reaching Keet Seel Ruin, this hike is worthwhile just for the sheer beauty of the canyon. Most of the route traverses Navajo land, so it is not uncommon to encounter small flocks of sheep and goats or perhaps glimpse a Navajo riding his horse to or from his hogan or traditional home.

Except for a short, steep, sandy stretch near the trailhead, the trail is mainly level and simply follows the canyon bottom. High walls of Navajo and Kayunta sandstones stand guard over the creek bed. As the trail meanders up the canyon, you pass plants typical of the plateau country four-wing saltbush, big sagebrush, virgin's bower, Mormon tea, rabbitbrush, snake-wood, pinyon pine, and juniper. You may also notice potshards, worked stone, or other artifacts of the Anasazi sticking out of the sandy trail. Please enjoy these treasures and leave them for future visitors.

It is necessary to obtain a permit from the park service at Navajo National Monument.

To reach the trailhead, turn off U.S. 163 onto Arizona 564 about 20 miles southwest of Kayenta. Drive 10 miles to Navajo National Monument and pick up your permit. The park rangers will tell you how to locate the trailhead and where to park your car.

At Keet Seel Ruin there is a primitive campground for overnight hikers but no water. Any water that you may find along the way is highly suspect and should only be used if you can treat it properly.—*Stewart Aitchison*

HIKE 35 *WHITE HOUSE RUIN*

General description: A short round-trip day hike to one of the Southwest's most striking cliff dwellings.
General location: Seven miles east of Chinle.
Maps: Three Turkey Canyon 7.5-minute, Del Muerto 7.5-minute USGS quads.
Difficulty: Easy.
Length: 1.25 miles one way.
Elevation: 6,000 to 5,500 feet.
Special attractions: Cliff dwellings, incredible sandstone canyons, and glimpses of Navajo Reservation life.
Best season: Anytime, although spring run-off and summer flooding occasionally make the crossing of Chinle Creek impossible.
For more information: Canyon de Chelly National Monument, Box 588, Chinle, AZ 86503; (520) 674-5510.

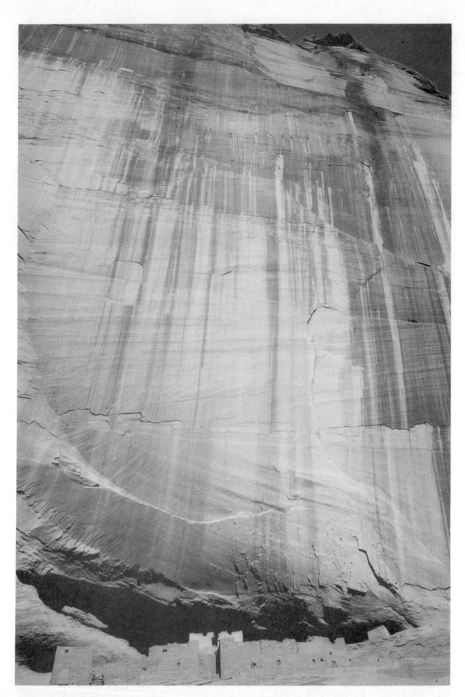

White House Ruin in Canyon de Chelly is a well-preserved Anasazi site. Above the ruin are long, black streaks of desert varnish staining the sandstone cliff. Desert varnish, or patina, is a surface deposit of manganese or iron oxide. It usually forms where water periodically washes down the cliff, but the exact processes involved are still poorly understood. Bruce Grubbs

Permit: None required but you must stay on the trail.
Wilderness status: None.

The hike: This is the only trail in Canyon de Chelly National Monument that you may hike without a local guide. To reach the trailhead, take the South Rim drive from the monument visitor center on the east side of Chinle. After about 6.4 miles, turn left into the White House Overlook parking lot.

The trail begins about 150 yards to your right as you face the canyon. The trail switchbacks down about 500 vertical feet to the canyon floor opposite and just upstream from White House Ruin, named after the white plaster walls of the upper portion of the ruin. Plan twice as much time to return to the rim as it took you to descend.

This ruin, which is your turnaround point, consists of rooms built in the cave and a multi-storied masonry pueblo below. Access to the cave was by ladders from the rooftops of the lower pueblo. Perhaps fifty or more people lived in this village from approximately 1040 A.D. to 1275 A.D. They planted maize, squash, and beans along the canyon bottom much like the Navajo people do today, and they gathered wild fruits and nuts and hunted rabbits.—
Stewart Aitchison

HIKE 36 *EAST POCKET TRAIL*

General description: A round-trip day hike into the Red Rock-Secret Mountain Wilderness Area.
General location: About mid-way through Oak Creek Canyon; about 9 miles north of Sedona on U.S. 89A.
Maps: Wilson Mountain 7.5-minute, Munds Park 7.5-minute USGS quads; Coconino National Forest map.
Difficulty: Easy.
Length: 2.5 miles to East Pocket Fire Lookout.
Elevation: 5,160 to 7,200 feet.
Special attractions: Splendid views of Oak Creek Canyon and surrounding Red Rock-Secret Mountain Wilderness Area; solitude.
Water availabilty: None once you leave Oak Creek.
Best season: Spring and fall. Crossing Oak Creek may be impossible during spring runoff.
For more information: Sedona Ranger District, P.O. Box 300, Sedona, AZ 86336; (520) 282-4119.
Permit: None.

The hike: Although the upper switchbacks of this trail are visible from one of Arizona's busiest (albeit spectacular) highways, it is rarely hiked. The majority of the 2.5 million annual visitors to Oak Creek Canyon seem to prefer to enjoy the canyon either from their autos or by sipping a few cool ones down by the creek.

For the hiker, Oak Creek Canyon and the surrounding rim country offer a variety of adventures.

In the 1870s, '80s, and '90s, homesteaders began to settle in the canyon. Since travel through the canyon was hampered by thick vegetation and numerous stream crossings, most of these early settlers built trails from their homes to the rim of the canyon. At the top they would leave their wagons and only bring their livestock and supplies down the trail.

The East Pocket Trail was originally built as a cattle trail to move animals up to the Ponderosa pine forest beyond the rim. In the 1930s, the Civilian Conservation Corps improved the trail.

The Red Rock-Secret Mountain Wilderness is one of Arizona's most accessible. Stewart Aitchison

To locate the trailhead, park at the Bootlegger Campground, which is about 9 miles north of Sedona on U.S. 89 A. During the spring and fall this campground is closed but you can park along the highway. Walk through the campground and descend the steep bank to Oak Creek. Unless the creek is unusually high, you can find stepping stones that allow you to cross with dry feet.

On the west side of the creek, a definite trail runs parallel to the stream. Depending on exactly where you crossed, the East Pocket Trail will branch off this trail either a few hundred feet upstream or downstream. Don't be fooled by faint game paths leading uphill. The East Pocket Trail is a clearly defined trail marked by a Forest Service sign where it begins its upward climb to the rim, and it marks one of Arizona's newest (1984) designated wilderness areas, the Red Rock-Secret Mountain Wilderness Area.

The ascent to the rim takes you through a thick stand of chaparral vegetation.

The common plants include scrub live oak, mountain mahogany, silk-tassel bush, and manzanita. Banana and narrow-leaf yucca along with agave and prickly pear cactus make a formidable barrier to off-trail walking. Once on top, the vegetation makes a dramatic change to ponderosa pine forest with alligator-bark juniper and Gambel's oak along the forest edge.

Side-blotched, tree, and fence lizards are common in the chaparral, as are rufous-sided towhees. Gray-collared chipmunks, Steller's jays, and even black bears roam the pine forest.

At the rim, follow the remainder of the trail west to the East Pocket Fire Lookout, your turnaround point. Watch for faint tree blazes marking the way along the rim.

There are great views off the rim into Oak Creek Canyon, to the north of the San Francisco Peaks, and to the south into the Verde Valley. Hardy explorers may be able to find an exciting climbing route to the north into the West Fork of Oak Creek.—*Stewart Aitchison* □

Oak Creek
Canyon

Hill Road

89A

Sedona

Schnebly

89A

Munds
Mtn.

Jacks Canyon Trail

Subdivision

NORTH

Village of
Oak Creek

FR 793

Jacks Canyon

179

One Mile

HIKE 37 *JACK'S CANYON*

General description: A round-trip day hike in Munds Mountain Wilderness Area.

General location: About a mile east of Oak Creek Village.

Maps: Munds Mountain 7.5-minute quad; Coconino National Forest map.

Difficulty: Moderate.

Length: About seven miles one way.

Elevation: 4,200 to 6,400 feet.

Special attractions: A walk up a rough canyon, fine views of lower Oak Creek.

Water availability: None.

Best season: March through November.

For more information: Sedona Ranger District, P.O. Box 300, Sedona, AZ 86336; (520) 282-4119.

Permit: None.

The hike: Take Arizona 179 to the village of Oak Creek (south of Sedona), and turn east on Jack's Canyon Road (Forest Road 793). Stay on Forest Road 793, which becomes dirt. The road ends in a subdivision. Park at the cattleguard at the entrance to this subdivision. The Jack's Canyon Trail begins as a jeep trail forking right just before this cattleguard. The jeep trail ends at Jack's Canyon Tank about 1.5 miles from the main road (also the Wilderness boundary). Forest Trail 55 continues up the canyon approximately four miles to the saddle between Munds Mountain and the Mogollon Rim. Trail 55 turns right and climbs a short distance to the Rim. Trail 77 goes left from the saddle and climbs to the gentle summit of Munds Mountain. From either of these points, return the way you came.

The entire saddle area offers fine views of lower Oak Creek Canyon and the Schnebly Hill area. The trail begins in typical chaparral scrub, consisting mainly of scrub oak, mountain mahogany, and manzanita. The higher parts of Jack's Canyon support a pinyon-juniper forest woodland while Munds Mountain is topped by ponderosa pine.—*Bruce Grubbs*

HIKE 38 *SECRET MOUNTAIN*

General description: An overnight round-trip backpack into the heart of the Red Rock-Secret Mountain Wilderness Area.

General location: Ten miles northwest of Sedona.

Maps: Loy Butte 7.5-minute, Wilson Mtn. 7.5-minute USGS quads; Coconino National Forest map.

Difficulty: Moderate.

Length: Five miles to the top of Secret Mountain; an additional 1-3 miles for the best views.

Elevation: 4,720 to 6,400 feet.

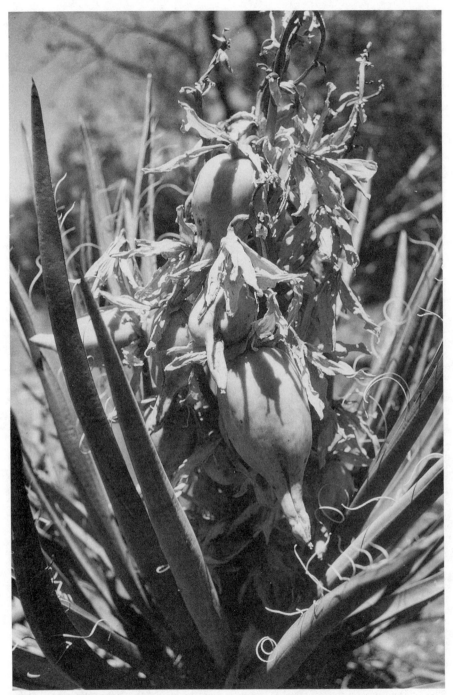

Yuccas are occasionally mistaken for cactus but are really members of the lily family. This is a banana yucca, so called because of its large, edible fruit. The Southwestern Indians, past and present, used the yucca plant for food, fiber, beverage, soap, and even as a laxative. Stewart Aitchison

What is the secret of Secret Mountain? One legend says outlaws stayed at this old cabin atop the mountain, while another legend says Mormon polygamists hid out here in the 1880s. Stewart Aitchison

Special attractions: Great views of the Red Rock Country from the top of Secret Mountain; solitude.
Water availability: Small springs on summit of Secret Mountain; may be dry in late summer.
Best season: Spring, summer, fall.
For more information: Sedona Ranger District, P.O. Box 300, Sedona, AZ 86336; (520) 282-4119.
Permit: None.

The hike: To locate the trailhead, drive about ten miles west of Sedona on U.S. 89A and then turn right onto Forest Road 525. Take the right fork after 2.7 miles and the left fork after 5.7 miles. There is a sign here that reads, "Loy Butte—4 miles." At 9.2 miles from the highway and just before you cross a tree-lined wash, there is a small Forest Service sign on your right marking the Loy Canyon Trail. There is a parking area across the road to your left.

The Loy Canyon Trail will take you to the saddle connecting Secret Mountain and the main Mogollon Rim. From the saddle, the Secret Mountain Trail wanders out along the summit of the mountain through a ponderosa pine forest with exciting views of the Red Rock Country and the Verde Valley.

The trail begins in desert scrub consisting of catclaw acacia, Arizona cypress, shrub live oak, narrowleaf and banana yucca, beargrass, and prickly pear cactus. The trail soon begins to follow a usually dry wash and the vegetation becomes more dense; alligator-bark juniper, mock orange, Virginia creeper, Arizona grape, and manzanita appear.

About .75 miles from the trailhead, you will see several small cliff dwellings in the alcove to the west.

These were built by the Sinaquans, a prehistoric agrarian people that occupied the Red Rock Country during the twelfth and thirteenth centuries.

As you continue up the trail, plants more typical of the forested rim area make their appearance; these include ponderosa pine, Douglas fir, white fir, buckbrush, cliffrose, and Gambel's oak. At about mile 3.5, the trail begins to switchback up through chaparral vegetation. You pass from the red Supai Formation, through the buff, cross-bedded Coconino Sandstone, and then contour through the gray Kaibab Limestone.

At the head of Loy Canyon, you reach the saddle connecting Secret Mountain with the main plateau. The adventuresome can bushwhack down into the upper reaches of Secret Canyon. Most hikers, though, will prefer heading south along the trail out to viewpoints on Secret Mountain. Along the way you will pass several small tanks that generally contain water and the remains of Secret Cabin, where there is a small spring.

In the 1870s, Samuel Loy and his son James homesteaded in Loy Canyon. Unfortunately a drought during the 1880s forced them to relocate. During the late 1800s, this area was used by outlaws as a hideout. One story relates how horse rustlers brought stolen horses to the top of Secret Mountain, changed their brands, then took them to Utah, Colorado, or New Mexico to be sold.—*Stewart Aitchison* □

Taylor Cabin deep in the Sycamore Canyon Wilderness is unique in that its back wall is a sandstone cliff. According to legend, somewhere nearby is a lost Spanish gold mine. The entrance to the mine is supposedly marked by a large meteorite. Stewart Aitchison.

HIKE 39 *SYCAMORE PASS-MOONEY LOOP*

General description: Two-to-three-day loop backpack through the Sycamore Canyon Wilderness and the Red Rock-Secret Mountain Wilderness areas.

General location: Twelve miles north of Cottonwood.

Maps: Loy Butte 7.5-minute, Sycamore Point 7.5-minute, Clarkdale 7.5-minute USGS quads; Coconino National Forest map.

Difficulty: Moderate.

Length: About twenty-one miles round trip.

Elevation: 4,300 to 6,400 feet.

Special attractions: Red rock canyons; solitude; wildlife.

Water availability: Seasonal water in Sycamore Creek and Mooney (Spring) Creek.

Best season: Spring and fall.

For more information: Sedona Ranger District, P.O. Box 300, Sedona, AZ 86336; (520) 282-4119.

Permits: None.

The hike: This two-to-three-day backpack takes you into two of the most beautiful areas of northern Arizona, the Sycamore Canyon Wilderness Area and the Red Rock-Secret Mountain Wilderness Area.

To find the trailhead, drive northeast out of Cottonwood toward Sedona on U.S. 89A. About nine miles from Cottonwood turn left onto Forest Road 525.

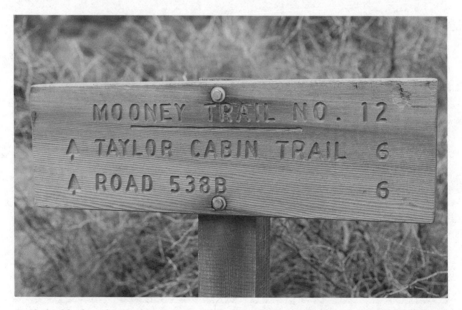

Look for black or brown hairs stuck on the rough edges of Forest Service trail signs such as this one in the Sycamore Canyon Wilderness Area. Black bear sometimes use these signs as scratching posts. Stewart Aitchison

NORTH

In 2.7 miles take the left fork, Forest Road 525C. Follow this road to its end at Sycamore Pass, a distance of about twelve miles.

The trail begins here among the red Supai and tan Coconino sandstone cliffs and is rocky as it descends from the pass into the Sycamore Wilderness Area and skirts through a pinyon-juniper woodland. It is easy to follow since it appears to have been a jeep road prior to becoming a foot trail. In about five miles the trail reaches the Sycamore Creek bed, which is usually dry although isolated pools may exist. After another .5 mile, you intersect the Sycamore Basin Trail coming from the southwest wilderness boundary. Check your topo map often, since the trail junction is not signed. Continue northeast, parallelling Sycamore Creek.

In about three miles you will come to Taylor Cabin, a cowboy line shack built in 1931. In the front wall are the carved brands of four ranches which have used it. Also here are the names of the stone masons who built the cabin, Despain and Porter. The cabin is a designated National Historic Site. There are often pools of water in the creek bed near the cabin but these, too, can dry up by the end of summer.

Wildlife is abundant in the canyon. Tracks of javelina, mule deer, whitetail deer, and ringtail cats can be found. Rock squirrels and pack rats live around the cabin.

The trail continues upstream from Taylor Cabin two miles and then forks. The left branch goes another mile before exiting the canyon and passing Ott Lake and Winter Cabin. Your route, however, follows the right fork and climbs 1,800 vertical feet within two miles to Buck Ridge.

At the ridge, the trail crosses an old jeep road which follows a power line. You can follow this old road south to Casner Mountain and eventually back to Sycamore Pass. This way back to your car is about 7 miles and offers spectacular views of the San Francisco Peaks, Sycamore Canyon, the Verde Valley, and the Red Rock country.

Another alternative is to cross Buck Ridge and drop into Mooney Canyon via the fairly good horse trail. About .5 mile after reaching the canyon floor, the trail crosses the dry creek west to east. Here is a lovely grotto and arch carved into the Supai Sandstone. Javelina are common in this area, too, where the thick chaparral vegetation provides cover and one of their favorite foods, prickly pear cactus, is abundant.

After about 4.5 miles from Buck Ridge, the trail becomes fainter and confused by cow paths. Don't fret—just continue down the canyon on the most definite path until the canyon opens up, where you will be within a few hundred feet to the west of the jeep road shown on the Loy Butte quad. To return to Sycamore Pass either follow the jeep road 525B to Black Tank and then walk up 525C, or else contour around to the southwest until you encounter road 525C. This second choice can be brushy but does save you a couple of miles.—*Stewart Aitchison* □

HIKE 40 GERONIMO SPRINGS

General description: A round-trip day hike or overnight trip in the remote upper end of the Sycamore Canyon Wilderness Area.

General location: About seventeen miles southeast of Flagstaff.

Maps: Sycamore Point 7.5-minute USGS quad; Coconino National Forest map.

Difficulty: Moderate.

Length: Three miles one way.

Elevation: 6,800 to 5,200 feet.

Special attractions: Elk, black bear, mule deer; solitude; a deep, narrow canyon.

Water availability: Several springs.

Best season: Late spring through fall.

For more information: Peaks Ranger District, 5075 N. Hwy 89, Flagstaff, AZ 86004; (520) 526-0866.

Permit: None.

The hike: To reach the beginning of this delightful hike, drive out of Flagstaff on the Turkey Butte Road (Forest 231) on the west end of town on Old Route 66. The Turkey Butte Road turns off just west of the Kit Carson Trailer Park. About 18 miles from the highway, take Forest Road 538 for 4.5 miles. Then turn right onto 538E. Follow this to its end in 1.5 mile. The maze of roads near the canyon is confusing, but by using the Forest Service map in conjunction with the topo quad you should be able to stay on the right course. Generally this route is passable to two-wheel drive vehicles with good clearance, but do not attempt it if there has been a lot of rain recently.

From the end of the road, the signed trail takes off downhill through a ponderosa pine forest. Wild turkey and deer are common. In a little over a mile you reach Dorsey Spring, which is permanent. The trail forks here. The left branch contours south toward Winter Cabin and other trails leading to Sycamore Canyon. (The ruin of Winter Cabin is the unnamed black square at the spring shown in the extreme northeast corner of section 14 on the USGS quad.) The right fork is your route.

Another 1.5 miles through the pines brings you to Babes Hole Spring, another dependable water source. The last .5 mile of trail to Geronimo Springs, your turnaround point, descends rapidly to the canyon floor.

Watch for elk in this area, as well as black bear tracks.—*Stewart Aitchison*

× 5160

Geronimo Spg.

Kelsey Spg.
× 6600

FR 527 A

○ *Babes Hole Spring*

FR 538 G

Sycamore Canyon

× 6800 FR 538E

○ *Dorsey Spring*

🐾 Hog Hill

One Mile

Winter Cabin Spring ○

□ *Winter Cabin*

🪶 *Ott Lake*

NORTH

HIKE 41 *BELL TRAIL*

General description: A round-trip day hike or easy overnight into The Wet Beaver Wilderness Area.
General location: About 2.5 miles east of the Sedona exit on Interstate 17.
Maps: Casner Butte 7.5-minute USGS quad; Coconino National Forest map.
Difficulty: Easy.
Length: About 3 miles one way (to junction of Long Canyon).
Elevation: 3,800 to 4,100 feet.
Special attractions: Spectacular, rugged canyon; permanent stream.
Water: Permanent stream.
Best season: April through November.
For more information: Beaver Creek Ranger District, HC 64, Box 240, Rimrock, AZ 86335; (520) 567-4501.
Permit: None.

The hike: From Interstate 17 in the Verde Valley, take the Sedona Exit (Arizona 179) but turn east onto Forest Road 618. Drive about two miles and turn east at the sign for Wet Beaver Creek. Park after .25 mile at the trailhead. Trail 13, the Bell Trail, begins as an old jeep trail. After about two miles it becomes a foot trail, and just before this point the unsigned Apache Maid Trail climbs away from Wet Beaver Creek to the north. The Bell Trail continues to skirt the north side of the creek, following the running stream with its fine swimming holes and lush riparian vegetation (including poison ivy—beware!). After about a mile, there are several good campsites. At this point the Bell Trail crosses the creek to the south and climbs southeast to the canyon rim where there are fine views of the area. This makes a good turnaround point for the hike.—*Bruce Grubbs*

Editors Note: For Bell Trail Map see Hikes 7 & 8, page 30.

HIKE 42 *WEST CLEAR CREEK*

General description: Two-day or longer loop backpack (and swim) through the West Clear Creek Wilderness Area.
General location: Twelve miles east of Camp Verde.
Maps: Calloway Butte 7.5-minute, Buckhorn Mountain 7.5-minute USGS quads; Coconino National Forest map.
Difficulty: Moderate to difficult (cross-country).
Length: Nine miles round trip.
Elevation: 6,650 to 5,200 feet.
Special attractions: A permanent clear water stream with great swimming holes.
Water availability: Clear stream and springs; best to purify.
Best season: Summer and early fall.

For more information: Long Valley Ranger District, HC-31, Box 68, Happy Jack, AZ 86024; (520) 354-2480, 345-2216.
Permit: None.

The hike: This backpack is challenging because the "trail" is mostly the creek and there are several places where you must swim to continue down the canyon. But it is well worth every effort. Just as you think the canyon with its soaring Coconino Sandstone walls couldn't be lovelier, you round the corner and the cold trout stream jumps off into a crystal clear pool so deep that you can barely discern the bottom.

There are a number of ways into and out of the canyon. This hike description is for the central, more remote section. To find the trailhead, turn off of the General Crook Trail (Forest Highway 9) onto Forest Road 144. This is about 3 miles from the junction of the General Crook Trail and Arizona 87. After about 2 miles, turn left onto Forest Service Route 149. Proceed to Route 142 and turn left. About 4.5 miles later you will see New Tank on your right. Park here.

Hiking often turns into swimming in West Clear Creek. Some backpackers pack their gear in a heavyweight plastic bag, which traps enough air to buoy a backpack. Other hikers bring along a small vinyl raft or inner tube. But beware of flash floods, particularly during the thunderstorm season of July and August. Stewart Aitchison

West Clear Creek

Route

5800'

4 WD

6200'

NORTH

Transmission Line

5700'

Trail

6300'

Bueno
Tank

Tule Butte

FR 142 B
4WD

FR 142 A

New Tank

6700'

FR 142

6860'
Calloway
Butte

One Mile

Overlooking the West Clear Creek Wilderness, this Parry agave is in full bloom. Agaves are also called century plants because they wait many years, usually from eight to thirty years, before sending up a stalk and flowering. After this one blooming, the plant dies. The fermented pulp of a Mexican species of agave produces the fiery beverage tequila. Stewart Aitchison

Follow Forest Road 142B, which is the jeep trail leading northward from the east side of New Tank. In about 2 miles you will come to a fence on the rim of West Clear Creek. Just to your left is a small gate which leads you to a short, steep trail to the canyon floor.

If you are feeling lazy, this idyllic spot can be your goal. Lush vegetation lines the stream; ponderosa pine, Douglas fir, and white fir cover the canyon walls. In their cool shade, Virginia creeper, New Mexico locust, bigtooth maple, and Arizona grape thrive. Crayfish and trout lurk in the watery shadows, trying to avoid becoming a meal for a nearby belted kingfisher. A mule deer crashes through the brush while a broad-tailed hummingbird whirs to a brilliant scarlet penstemon flowering along the creek.

If you can tear yourself away, more spectacular sites await downstream.

You must follow the topographic map carefully or else the sinuous winding of the canyon will disorient you and finding the correct exit will be difficult.

The five miles or so to your exit point can be traveled in a strenuous day, but there are so many wonderful swimming spots that two or even three days is not unreasonable. Most of your walking will be in water calf- or knee-deep, but there are several spots where swimming will be necessary. This hike should not be undertaken in spring or early summer when high runoff and cold water could mean hypothermia. And during the thunderstorm season of July and August, flash floods may occur, so exercise caution.

Some hikers have solved the "pool crossing" problem by bringing lightweight one-person rafts to put their packs in. Others put their belongings in water-proof rubber bags which in turn fit inside their packs. Enough air is trapped inside the bags to make the backpacks float reasonably well. But even in August the water can be chilly.

As you travel downstream, you will notice that the character of the canyon changes. In places the stream is clogged with massive gray basalt boulders, a particularly tedious part of the trip as you attempt to hop from rock to rock. Other stretches of the canyon are enclosed by soaring sandstone cliffs and the stream spreads out across a sandstone bed nearly as flat as a sidewalk.

About four miles downstream from the entry point, you pass through a .75-mile relatively straight stretch of canyon trending to the northwest. You then arrive at another falls and a long pool that must be swum. After this the stream turns to the south (more or less). Your exit route is located about .3 mile farther, just before the canyon narrows again and the stream begins a series of steep drops. But if you have the time, slip off your pack and continue downstream another .25 mile. Here you will find some of the deepest and longest pools of the entire canyon, one of which is 100 yards long with sheer cliffs plunging into the water.

Back at the exit route, you will notice several faint game trails leading upward, and the Coconino National Forest map indicates the presence of Trail 40. However, I have never been able to locate Trail 40, so just head uphill through the chaparral. It's only a few hundred yards to the rim and if you choose your route carefully, you can avoid most of the prickly, scratchy vegetation. At the rim, walk easterly a few hundred yards and you will cross the jeep track that leads four miles back to New Tank.

If you have two four-wheel drive vehicles, you can also arrange a shuttle by leaving one of them closer to the rim, saving you as much as six miles of walking.—*Stewart Aitchison* □

HIKE 43 *CHEVELON CANYON*

General description: A two- or three-day backpacking trip, out and back.
General location: Forty miles south of Winslow.
Maps: Chevelon Crossing 7.5-minute USGS quad; Apache-Sitgreaves National Forest map.
Difficulty: Moderate.
Length: About ten miles one way.
Elevation: 6,300 to 7,000 feet.
Special attractions: Beaver are common in Chevelon Creek.
Water availability: Chevelon Creek is permanent.
Best season: Spring through fall.
For more information: Chevelon Ranger District, HC 61, Box 1, Winslow, AZ, 86047; (520) 289-3381.
Permit: None.

The hike: This is a delightful backpack into a forested canyon containing one of Arizona's rarest resources, a permanent trout stream. Drive south out of Winslow on Arizona 99 for approximately thirty-eight miles to Chevelon Crossing and campground. .

From here, it is about a ten-mile hike upstream to Chevelon Canyon Lake, a manmade reservoir which is your turnaround point. Along the way are beaver ponds, swimming holes, and grassy campsites amid ponderosa pine, cottonwood, locust, and other riparian species. There is no formal trail but it is possible to walk along the canyon floor, following game and livestock paths, without too many stream crossings. Elk and deer are common.

Exploration downstream is also possible but somewhat more difficult. The canyon narrows, and more time is necessary to cross or even sometimes swim confluence with the Little Colorado River, but were turned back about halfway there by a massive barrier of floating logs. It was impossible to walk across them or around them, and the canyon walls at that spot were unclimbable.

In 1851, Captain Lorenzo Sitgreaves wrote that the stream received its name from a trapper called Chevalon who died after eating some poisonous root along its bank. Poison hemlock does grow along the creek, and may well have been the culprit.—*Stewart Aitchison*

To Winslow

99

FR 504

Chevelon Crossing Campground

Chevelon Creek

6400' × Ⓟ

To Heber

NORTH

× Dam

←*Chevelon Lake* 6800'

One Mile

Upper Chevelon Canyon is wide enough that hiking along the creek bank is feasible. Downstream, however, the canyon narrows and swimming becomes necessary. Poison ivy and the thorny New Mexican locust are also common along the creek, so watch your step.—Stewart Aitchison

HIKE 44 *ABINEAU CANYON-REESE CANYON*

General description: A loop day hike in the Kachina Peaks Wilderness Area.
General location: North slopes of the San Francisco Peaks, north of Flagstaff.
Maps: Humphreys Peak 7.5-minute, White Horse Hills 7.5-minute USGS quads; Coconino National Forest map.
Difficulty: Moderate.
Length: About eight miles.
Elevation: 8,250 to 10,400 feet.
Special attractions: Alpine forest of fir and aspen, views of north slopes of Humphreys Peak.
Water availability: Snow early season, otherwise none.
Best season: June through October.
For more information: Peaks Ranger District, 5075 N. Hwy 89, Flagstaff, AZ 86004, (520) 526-0866.
Permit: None.

The hike: Drive about eighteen miles north of Flagstaff on U.S. 180, then turn east onto Forest Road 151. After approximately 1.5 miles, turn left onto Forest Road 418. In about four miles, turn right (south) at the Aubineau Trail sign and onto a rough road, which leads .25 mile to Reese Tanks. Park at a locked gate then walk up the old road.

Just south (uphill) from the stock tanks, follow a badly eroded jeep trail up the gradual slope. In about .5 mile, the old road forks; take the right fork (the left fork leads to the Reese Trail). After several hundred yards the Aubineau Trail forks right from the road and contours west into Aubineau Canyon. Do not continue on the jeep trail—it dead ends.

The trail continues up the bed of the canyon for approximately two miles. At the lower end, the forest is primarily ponderosa pine. Watch for especially large, old trees, a sign that the area has never been heavily logged. Gradually the ponderosas thin out as aspen, limber pine, and then fir and spruce take over at increasing elevations. The trail ends at the Aubineau Canyon road at 10,400 feet in a large meadow with a fine view of the north ridge of Humphreys Peak.

Although it would be possible to climb from here to the summit, the Forest Service has forbidden off-trail hiking above timberline because of the fragile nature of the tundra and the existence of a endemic alpine plant, the San Francisco Peaks Groundsel, which is threatened with extinction.

Note several unforested chutes running down into the meadow from the north ridge of Humphreys. These are active avalanche pat hs during the winter. There are enough large avalanches to keep the area at the end of the trail and about .25 mile down the canyon completely cleared of trees.

It is possible to make a loop trip by continuing east on the Abineau Canyon road about 2.5 miles to the Reese Trail. As you walk, you will first cross Reese Canyon, and then Bearjaw Canyon. About .5 mile past Bearjaw, watch for the unmarked trail dropping down the gentle slope to the north. Follow this trail as it continues down a gentle slope covered with aspens, then turns le ft and crosses Bearjaw Canyon. Occasional cairns mark the trail through a confusing maze of old logging roads as it continues northwest toward Reese Tanks. After

The higher slopes of the San Francisco Peaks comprise the Kachina Peaks Wilderness Area. A popular trail which begins at the Arizona Snowbowl ski lodge climbs the highest summit, Humphreys Peak at 12,670 feet. The Aubineau-Reese Canyon loop described in this guide, will get you away from the crowds. Stewart Aitchison

crossing Reese Canyon, the trail ends at the old jeep trail mentioned above. Follow the road back to Reese Tanks and your vehicle.

The Aubineau Trail is a recent extension of an old jeep trail which climbed part-way up the canyon. The Reese Trail is an old sheepherder's trail which has recently been improved. Increasing hiker and horse traffic will probably keep both trails distinct.

The Forest Service has established a trail system around the San Francisco Peaks including a good trail to the summit, Humphreys Peak. Contact either the Coconino National Forest Supervisor's Office or the Peaks Ranger District Office for information and maps.—*Bruce Grubbs*

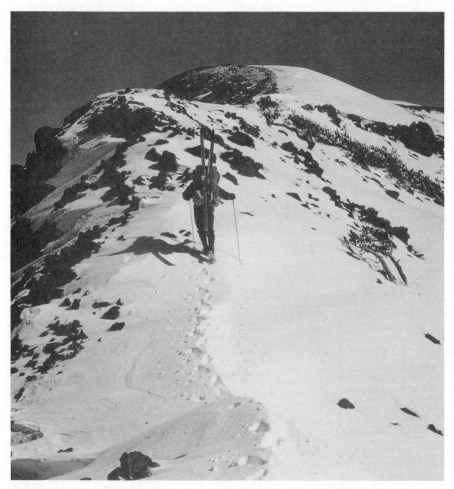

Near the top of Arizona, Humphreys Peak in the Kachina Peaks Wilderness Area—here shown on an early March hike and ski—averages more than two hundred inches of snow each winter. Stewart Aitchison

Reese
Tanks

FR 418

Potato Tank

Aubineau Canyon

Reese Trail

Bearjaw Canyon

NORTH

Aubineau Trail

Reese Canyon

Road Closed
To Vehicles

× 11474

× 11838

× 11783

San Francisco Peaks

Humphreys Peak
× 12670

One Mile

HIKE 45 *SLATE MOUNTAIN*

General description: A round-trip day hike in forest northwest of the San Francisco Peaks.

General location: Thirty miles north of Flagstaff.

Maps: Kendrick Peak 7.5-minute quad; Coconino National Forest map.

Difficulty: Easy.

Length: About two miles one way.

Elevation: 7,450 to 8,200 feet.

Special attractions: Pleasant and easy ascent to fine views of San Francisco volcanic field.

Water availability: None.

Best season: May through October.

For more information: Peaks Ranger Station, 5075 N. Hwy 89, Flagstaff, AZ 86004, (520) 526-0866.

Permit: None.

Wilderness status: None.

The hike: Drive about twenty-six miles north of Flagstaff on U.S. 180, then turn west on Forest Road 191. The Slate Mountain trail is signed and is approximately two miles from the highway. Drivers of low-clearance vehicles may wish to avoid the last .25 mile of road.

The trail is obvious and easy to follow, switchbacking up south slopes through pinyon-juniper woodland. Higher, the trail winds through ponderosa pine, then rounds the north side into Douglas fir. The view from the 8,215-foot summit, your turnaround point, is open and offers an expansive view of the northern slopes of the San Francisco Peaks and Kendrick Mountain, as well as Coconino Plateau.

Slate Mountain is an old cinder cone, one of several hundred located generally north of Flagstaff in the San Francisco volcanic field.

The Slate Mountain Trail is actually an old road, now closed to vehicles, which was used to service a fire lookout. The tower, along with several others on the north end of the forest, has long since been torn down.—*Bruce Grubbs*

HIKE 46 *LAVA RIVER CAVE*

General description: Round-trip day hike into a lava tube.
General location: Fifteen miles northwest of Flagstaff.
Maps: Coconino National Forest map.
Difficulty: Easy.
Length: Less than a mile round trip.
Elevation: 7,680 feet (no significant elevation change).
Special attractions: A unique geologic feature.
Water availability: None.
Best season: Spring through fall; winter, too, if you ski in.
For more information: Peaks Ranger Station, 5075 N. Hwy 89, Flagstaff, AZ 86004, (520) 526-0866.
Permit: None.
Wilderness status: None.

The hike: This is a different kind of hike—you explore the inside of a lava flow. When the molten rock began to cool, the interior of the flow continued to move, leaving a tube or cave in its wake.

To find the Lava River Cave, drive north out of Flagstaff on Arizona 180 about 13.5 miles and then turn left onto Forest Road 245. In about three miles you will come to a T-intersection, where you turn left onto Forest Road 171. Go just over a mile an d turn left, again, onto 171B (formerly 171A). A few hundred feet later, the road ends at the mouth of the cave.

Be sure each person in your party has at least two lights. It can get very dark in a lava tube. A Coleman-style lantern is a great illuminator. You may want to wear a hard hat.

The cave is quite different from solution caverns found in limestone. It contains no stalactites, stalagmites, or confusing labyrinths or side tunnels. Instead, it is just a single dead-end tunnel with a fairly rounded ceiling and rocky floor, almost like a primordial subway.—*Stewart Aitchison*

FS 171

FS 245

×7680

FS 171
A   Lava River Cave

Aspen Tank

180

×
7900

To
Flagstaff

NORTH

One Mile

HIKE 47 KENDRICK MOUNTAIN

General description: A round-trip day hike into Kendrick Mountain Wilderness Area.

General location: Twenty-five miles northwest of Flagstaff.

Maps: Kendrick Peak 7.5-minute USGS quad; Kaibab National Forest (South) map.

Difficulty: Moderate.

Length: Four miles one way.

Elevation: 8,000 to 10,400 feet.

Special attractions: Beautiful hike through alpine forest, superb views of San Francisco Peaks and the Coconino Plateau.

Water: Snow early season, otherwise none.

Best season: May through October.

For more information: Peaks Ranger Station, 5075 N. Hwy 89, Flagstaff, AZ 86004, (520) 526-0866.

Permit: None.

The hike: Drive about sixteen miles north from Flagstaff on U.S. 180, turn west onto Forest Road 193, and drive three miles west to Forest Road 171. Turn right (north) and drive about three miles to road 171A. This road ends at the signed trailhead in less than a mile.

Typically cloudless nights make tentless camping a real possibility in Arizona, but carry at least a tarp just in case. This prime campsite is located near the top of Kendrick Peak. Bruce Grubbs

The well-maintained trail climbs the south slopes of Kendrick Mountain. The lower part of the trail is a former jeep trail built to fight a fire on East Newman Hill many years ago. Higher, the trail switchbacks upward through stands of limber pine and aspen. Near the summit ridge, the forest changes to that typical of Southern Canada, with Engelmann spruce and Arizona corkbark fir. Just below the summit, the trail passes the old lookout cabin and the junction with the Bull Basin Trail. The final switchbacks lead to the summit cone and offer fine views to the south and east. A few yards from the lookout building, your turnaround point, the Pumpkin Center trail (see hike 48) branches off. If the lookout is home, he'll probably welcome the company. Just remember that the lookout building is his home and be sure to ask before climbing.—*Bruce Grubbs*

HIKE 48 *PUMPKIN CENTER*

General description: A round-trip day hike into Kendrick Mountain Wilderness Area.
General location: Thirty miles northwest of Flagstaff.
Maps: Kendrick Mountain 7.5-minute, Moritz Ridge 7.5-minute USGS quads; Kaibab National Forest (South) map.
Difficulty: Moderate.
Length: 4.5 miles one way.
Elevation: 7,200 to 10,400 feet.
Special attractions: Little-used trail with fine views enroute.
Water availability: Snow in early season, otherwise none.
Best season: May through October.
For more information: Williams Ranger District, Rt. 1, Box 142, Williams, AZ 86046, (520) 635-2633.
Permit: None.

The hike: Drive about 16 miles north from Flagstaff on U.S. 180, then turn west onto Forest Road 193. Drive three miles west to Forest Road 171, turn right (north), and drive about six miles to Pumpkin Center. A sign points out the trailhead.

The trail starts as an old logging road and climbs east up the side of Bull Basin Mesa for a little more than a mile, then be comes a foot trail and starts up the west ridge of Kendrick Mountain. You will pass the junction with the Connector Trail which connects to the Bull Basin Trail (see hike 49). The Pumpkin Trail continues up the ridge, steeply at times, while the forest changes from ponderosa pine to limber pine and aspen, alpine meadows and Douglas fir, and finally Engelmann spruce and bristlecone pine near the summit. There are excellent views to the west from the meadows.

The summit is the logical turnaround point on this hike, but you can also make this trek a loop by continuing down the Bull Basin Trail (see hike 49).—*Bruce Grubbs*

Bull
Basin 8050'

Bull Basin Trail

Connector Trail

Pumpkin
Center

Pumpkin

Center

Trail

Bear Spring

Mountain Spring

Cabin

10418'
Kendrick Peak

Kendrick

FR 171

NORTH

Kendrick Mountain Trail

8000'

FR 171 A

One Mile

FR 171

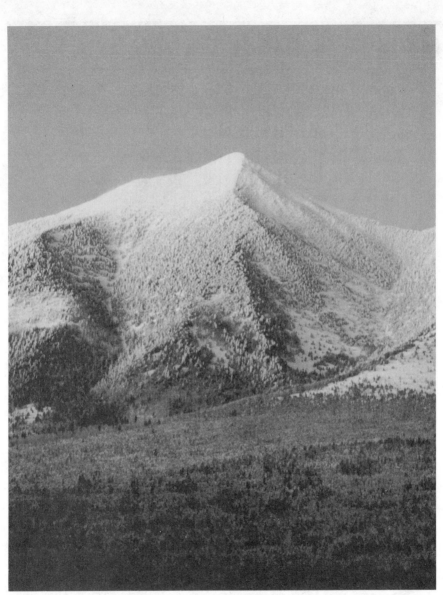

The San Francisco Peaks can be seen to the north of the White Horse Hills. Stewart Aitchison

HIKE 49 BULL BASIN

General description: A round-trip day hike in the Kendrick Mountain Wilderness Area.

General location: Forty miles northwest of Flagstaff.

Maps: Kendrick Mountain 7.5-minute, Moritz Ridge 7.5-minute USGS quads; Kaibab National Forest (South) map.

Difficulty: Moderate.

Length: 4.5 miles one way.

Elevation: 7,050 to 10,400 feet.

Special attractions: Little-used trail, loop with Pumpkin Center Trail.

Water availability: None.

Best season: May thru October.

For more information: Williams Ranger District, Rt. 1, Box 142, Williams, AZ 86046, (520) 635-2633.

Permit: None.

The hike: Drive about sixteen miles north from Flagstaff on U.S. 180, then turn west onto Forest Road 193. Drive three miles west to Forest Road 171, turn right (north), and drive about nine miles. Turn north (right) on Forest Road 144. Drive 1.25 miles, turn east (right) on Forest Road 90 and follow this road about 6 miles to the signed trailhead.

From the signed trailhead, the Bull Basin Trail climbs gradually up the north slopes of Kendrick Mountain through mixed pine, fir, and aspen. About .5 mile from the trailhead, you will reach the signed junction with the wilderness boundary trail. The Bull Basin Trail continues up the slope past Bear Spring (not reliable) and then ascends through fine fir forest to a saddle and open meadows bordered with aspen. Now the trail turns south and climbs to the old lookout cabin on the east ridge of Kendrick Mountain, where it joins the Kendrick Lookout Trail in an open meadow with hundred-mile views to the south. Continue on the Lookout Trail to reach the summit and the junction with the Pumpkin Center Trail. Then return the way you came, or return via the Pumpkin Center Trail to make this a loop hike.—*Bruce Grubbs*

HIKE 50 WHITE HORSE HILLS

General description: A round-trip day hike north of the San Francisco Peaks.

General location: Twenty miles north of Flagstaff.

Maps: White Horse Hills 7.5-minute USGS quad; Coconino National Forest map.

Difficulty: Easy.

Length: About a mile one way.

Elevation: 8,500 to 9,050 feet.

Special attractions: Close and spectacular views of Humphreys Peak.

Water availability: None.

Best season: May through November.

For more information: Peaks Ranger Station, 5075 N. Hwy 89, Flagstaff, AZ 86004, (520) 526-0866.
Permit: None.
Wilderness status: None.

The hike: Drive about eighteen miles north of Flagstaff on U.S. 180, then turn east onto Forest Road 151 (north Hart Prairie road). Drive east about two miles through beautiful stands of aspen and pine. Turn left (east) onto Forest Road 418. Drive east 2 miles to a large meadow with a stock tank and a cattleguard. This is Potato Tank Meadow.

The trail starts a few yards west at the highest point in the road. It is a former jeep trail which has been closed by the Forest Service. It ascends north to a saddle. From here it climbs along the slope to a higher saddle and forks. The left fork leads to the highest point of the White Horse Hills while the right fork leads to the east summit, which is only slightly lower. Both summits are turnaround points for this hike, both are approximately the same distance from the trailhead, and either offers excellent views of the northwest slopes of the San Francisco Peaks as well as the volcanic field to the north and west.

The White Horse Hills seem to be an old, badly eroded cinder cone, but there are some outcrops of Kaibab Limestone on the highest summit. This rock forms the general surface of the surrounding plateau, except where it is locally covered by cinders and lava. Perhaps large chunks of limestone were blasted loose during the eruption of the White Horse Hills and were carried up the vent to lodge near the surface.—*Bruce Grubbs* □

HIKE 51 *MOUNT ELDEN*

HIKE 51 *MOUNT ELDEN*

General description: A round-trip day hike in Flagstaff.
General location: East Flagstaff.
Maps: Flagstaff West 7.5-minute USGS quad; Coconino National Forest map.
Difficulty: Moderate.
Length: Three miles one way.
Elevation: 6,900 to 9,300 feet.
Water availability: None.
Best season: April through November.
For more information: Peaks Ranger Station, 5075 N. Hwy 89, Flagstaff, AZ 86004, (520) 526-0866.
Permit: None.
Wilderness status: None.

The hike: Drive to the Peaks Ranger Station in east Flagstaff on north highway 89. The marked turnoff to the trailhead is located along Santa Fe Avenue just north of the Ranger Station. Park at the signed trailhead.

The Elden Trail runs north along the east slopes of Mount Elden for about a mile before suddenly turning east and switchbacking steeply to the summit and your turnaround point. The forest is open and the views of east Flagstaff and the surrounding plateau are spectacular.

Little hint remains of the beautiful fir-aspen forest which thickly covered the summit before the Radio Fire in 1977. The fire was man-caused and started at the south base of the mountain on a hot and windy day. It spread explosively up the south slopes, across the summit area, and down the north and north-east slopes, and was only stopped at U.S. 89 after several days. Today one can clearly see the aspen beginning to prepare the way for a new fir forest, several hundred years in the future.

The summit area is reached by a road from the west, and a fire lookout and numerous radio towers crowd the top. A relatively new set of trails encircles Mount Elden. A map of this new Mount Elden-Dry Lake Hills Trail System is available at the Peaks Ranger Station.—*Bruce Grubbs*

HIKE 52 *STRAWBERRY CRATER*

General description: A short day hike in the Strawberry Crater Wilderness Area.
General location: Twenty miles northeast of Flagstaff.
Maps: Strawberry Crater 7.5-minute USGS quad; Coconino National Forest map.
Difficulty: Easy (cross-country).
Length: About .5 mile to rim of Strawberry Crater (no trail).
Elevation: 6,000 to 6,500 feet.
Special attractions: Recent and dramatic volcanic activity, rich archaeology.

Water availability: None.
Best season: Spring and fall.
For more information: Peaks Ranger Station, 5075 N. Hwy 89, Flagstaff, AZ 86004, (520) 526-0866.
Permit: None.

The hike: To reach the area, drive twelve miles north from Flagstaff on U.S. 89, then turn east (right) on the road to Sunset Crater (Forest Road 545, paved). Drive through the monument to Painted Desert Vista, about eight miles from U.S. 89. From here you can hike cross-country north and northeast into the cinder dune area of the Strawberry Crater Wilderness.

Another route begins about fifteen miles north of Flagstaff on U.S. 89. Turn east (right) on Forest Road 546, an unimproved dirt road. Drive about 3.5 miles to the junction with Forest Road 779, and take this road about two miles to the west base of Strawberry Crater. Do not drive off the road you can easily get stuck in the deep, loose cinders.

It is an easy cross-country walk to your turnaround point, the top of Strawberry Crater from the west base. The volcanic terrain is loose and jagged, and there is no trail. However, the view from the summit ridge is more than worth the climb. You can see the San Francisco Peaks to the southwest and the colorful Painted Desert and the Navajo Indian Reservation to the northeast.

Hiking around the base of Strawberry Crater and across the lava flow and cinder field is easier, although sturdy boots are valuable and gaitors may help keep pesky cinders out of your socks.

During the springtime and the summer monsoon months, many different flowers, grasses, and shrubs bloom, and wildlife is visible much of the year. A partial list of wildlife and vegetation commonly encountered on this hike includes mule deer, elk, coyote, several species of hawk, great horned owl, Townsend's solitaire, common flicker, plain titmouse, junco, western and mountain bluebird, one-seed juniper, pinyon pine, ponderosa pine, rubber paintbrush, Apache plume, desert olive, currant, phacelia, aster, California bricklebrush, skyrocket, and sand bluestem grass. One species, **penstemon clutei**, is found only in this area.

The area was home to the prehistoric Sinagua Indians 700-900 years ago. Pit houses used for temporary shelter during farming and hunting activities are numerous, and unique terraced garden areas in the cinders are still recognizable today. Walled structures in near-perfect condition remain in some parts of the area, which seems to have been used seasonally for farming by people who lived in the large, more permanent structures of nearby Wupatki National Monument. A few pueblos in the area may have been occupied year-round, as the climate allowed.

A visit to Wupatki and Sunset Crater national monuments before your hike will provide excellent cultural and geologic background information, making your visit more interesting and rewarding. Please remember to hike with care so as not to disturb any archaeological artifacts you may encounter. These sites are protected by law so their cultural and historical significance may be preserved for future generations. These valuable resources are extremely important to scientists, and may be irrevocably changed by disturbance.—*John Nelson*

West Cataroct Creek

To (40)

Williams

Old US 66

Perkinsville Road

Camp Clover
6915

Bill William Trail

Ski Area

×Bill William Mountain
9256'

×Bixler Mtn.

One Mile

NORTH

HIKE 53 *BILL WILLIAMS MOUNTAIN*

General description: A round-trip day hike on a forested volcano.
General location: About a mile west of Williams.
Maps: Williams South 7.5-minute USGS quad; Kaibab National Forest (South) map.
Difficulty: Moderate.
Length: Three miles one way.
Elevation: 6,900 to 9,250 feet.
Special attractions: Cool and shady walk up north-facing canyon, views of highcountry around Williams.
Water availability: None.
Best season: May through October.
For more information: Williams Ranger District, Rt.1, Box 142, Williams, AZ 86046;(520) 635-2633.
Permit: None.
Wilderness status: None.

The hike: From Williams, drive west on I-40 to the Camp Clover exit. Drive to Camp Clover (a Forest Service station) and park at the signed trailhead.

The trail ascends onto a bench covered with pinyon and juniper, then climbs into the cool, north-facing head of West Cataract Creek as the forest gives way to ponderosa pine, fir, and aspen. This drainage is part of the headwaters of Cataract Creek, which enters famous Havasu Canyon many miles to the north. The trail finally switchbacks up to end at the Bill Williams Road, which leads a short distance farther to the summit and your turnaround point. This trail is an excellent hike on a hot summer day.

The trail was built by the Forest Service for access to the fire tower on the summit before a road was built.—*Bruce Grubbs*

CENTRAL MOUNTAINS

Overview

From the Mogollon Rim south to the lower desert country is a band of rugged mountains and canyons. This area is a geologic transition zone between the Colorado Plateau and the Basin and Range country. It is also the most rugged part of the state. Hiking is possible year-round if one is careful about selecting the appropriate elevation for a particular season— canyons in colder seasons, mountain tops during the hot summer.

HIKE 54 *HELL'S GATE*

General description: An overnight or longer backpack into the Hell's Gate Wilderness Area.
General location: About eleven miles east of Payson.
Maps: Diamond Point 7.5-minute, McDonald Mountain 7.5-minute, Diamond Butte 7.5-minute USGS quads; Tonto National Forest map.
Difficulty: Difficult.
Length: About seven miles one way.
Elevation: 5,300 to 4,000 feet.
Special attractions: Cold, perennial trout streams.

HIKE 54 *HELL'S GATE*

Water availability: Only at Hell's Gate.
Best season: Spring and fall.
For more information: Payson Ranger District, P.O. Box 100, Payson, AZ 85541; (520) 474-7900.
Permit: None

The hike: To reach the trailhead, drive about eleven miles east of Payson on State Highway 260. Turn right onto Forest Road 405A just past Little Green Valley. Go about .3 mile and turn right at a cement water trough. The trailhead of Forest Service Trail 37 is located here.

This trail follows along Apache Ridge to the confluence of Haigler and Tonto creeks, a spectacular place known as Hell's Gate . Here canyon walls rise 1500 feet above the streams. Progress through the Haigler and Tonto Creek canyons is limited to those willing to navigate around rough, rock barriers and swim through deep pools.—*Tonto National Forest.*

HIKE 55 *HELL'S HOLE*

General description: A challenging backpack into the Salome Wilderness Area.
General location: Sixty miles northeast of Phoenix.
Maps: Aztec Peak 7.5-minute, Armor Mountain 7.5-minute, McFadden Peak 7.5-minute, Copper Mountain 7.5-minute USGS quads; Tonto National Forest map.
Difficulty: Difficult.
Length: 5.3 miles one way.
Elevation: 4,400 to 5,500 feet.
Special attractions: Deep, spectacular canyon.
Water availability: Workman Creek
Best season: Spring, fall, or winter.
For more information: Pleasant Valley Ranger District, P.O. Box 450, Young, AZ 85554; (520) 462-3311.
Permit: None.

The hike: To reach the east side of the Salome Wilderness Area, take State Highway 288 from Globe toward Young. Just south of the Reynolds Creek Campground is the trailhead for the Hell's Hole Trail 284. The trail climbs southwesterly to the pass between Jack Mountain and an un-named peak to the north. Beyond the pass, the trail drops into Workman Creek, which it crosses, and then climbs about 600 vertical feet. The trail passes just south of a knoll marked as 5682 on the topographic map and then drops steeply into Hell's Hole. As of spring, 1988, some of the trail was overgrown and downed trees made route finding challenging.

The determined angler can try his luck in Workman Creek for German brown and rainbow trout. Other wildlife that might be encountered includes mule deer, white-tailed deer, javelina, mountain lion, coyote, black bear, and wild turkey.—*Tonto National Forest.*

HIKE 56 *PINE MOUNTAIN*

General description: Two-day loop hike in the Pine Mountain Wilderness Area.

General location: Twenty-five miles east of Cordes Junction.

Maps: Tule Mesa 7.5-minute USGS quad; Prescott National Forest map.

Difficulty: Moderate.

Length: About seventeen miles.

Elevation: 5,200 to 6,800 feet.

Special attractions: Remote and little-hiked area, with excellent views of the wild parts of the Verde River and the Mazatzal Mountains.

Water availability: See description.

Best season: April through November.

For more information: Verde Ranger District, Box 670, Camp Verde, AZ 86322; (520) 567-4121.

Permit: None.

The hike: From I-17 north of Cordes Junction, take the Dugas Road exit and go east twenty-five miles to the road's end and the trailhead. This road (Forest Road 68) can be rough beyond Dugas. A high-clearance vehicle is recommended.

Pine Mountain is a small wilderness astride the Verde Rim offering super views of both the wild Verde River country south of Camp Verde and the north-western Mazatzal Mountains. If it weren't for a powerline corridor just outside the Pine Mountain Wilderness, the two areas could be joined into one wilderness.

From the signed road end at Nelson Place Spring (featuring good camping and water), it is possible to complete a loop hike over the highest point in the wilderness, Pine Mountain, in one long day or two easier days.

Walk about .25 mile up the trail along Sycamore Creek, then turn south on the signed Beehouse Canyon trail (Forest Trail 165) which climbs a mile to the head of Beehouse Canyon. Here the trail meets the signed Pine Flat Trail (Forest Trail 165). Turn southeast (left) toward Pine Flat. The trail crosses Pine Flat, a fine stand of Ponderosa pines, and continues south into the South Prong of Sycamore Creek, then climbs to meet the Verde Rim Trail in a saddle. Turn east (left) on the signed Verde Rim Trail (Forest Trail 59) which contours around to Bishop Creek. Bishop Spring is located in the drainage west of Bishop Creek and should be reliable.

At Bishop Creek, a signed trail (Forest Trail 159) offers a shortcut back to Sycamore Creek and the road head. Take the right fork southeast (Forest Trail 161) about a mile to the edge of the Verde Rim. The trail now turns northeast and climbs along the rim toward Pine Mountain. Some sections may be brushy. About .75 mile south of Pine Mountain, you pass the signed junction with Forest Trail 14. Forest Trail 161 continues through a fine pine grove, then passes just below the summit of Pine Mountain. The summit itself is easy to reach, though there is no trail, and is open with excellent 360-degree views.

North of Pine Mountain, Forest Trail 161 descends steeply to a saddle at the head of Sycamore Creek and the junction with the Willow Spring Trail. Turn west (left) on this trail. About .5 mile further on, there is seasonal water

NORTH

One Mile

and Willow Spring should be reliable. From here, it is an easy and pleasant walk along the trail down Sycamore Creek to the trailhead.—*Bruce Grubbs* □

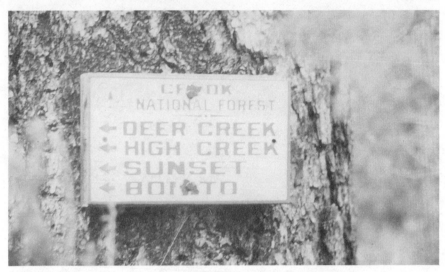

Traces of the past are common in the Mazatzal Wilderness. This old Forest Service sign predates 1953, when the Crook National Forest was divided into the Tonto, Coronado, and Gila national forests. Bruce Grubbs

HIKE 57 *DEER CREEK*

General description: Two- or three-day loop hike in the Mazatzal Wilderness Area.

General location: Twenty miles southwest of Payson.

Maps: Mazatzal Peak 7.5-minute USGS quad; USFS Mazatzal Wilderness map.

Difficulty: Moderate.

Length: About sixteen miles.

Elevation: 3,550 to 6,000 feet.

Special attractions: Little-used loop trail into the head of a forested canyon below fine peaks.

Water availability: Seasonal in Deer Creek, Windsor Camp.

Best season: September-November, April-May.

For more information: Payson Ranger District, P.O. Box 100, Payson, AZ 85541; (520) 474-7900.

Permit: None.

The hike: The Deer Creek Trailhead is probably the easiest Mazatzal trailhead to reach. It is only a few yards off a paved highway, yet is not heavily used. From Arizona 87, at the junction with Arizona 188, turn west on Forest Road 492. Drive to the new parking area at the trailhead.

Three trails start from this trailhead, all infrequently used. It is possible to use two of these trails as part of a fine overnight or three-day loop hike into the rugged and scenic country at the head of Deer Creek.

Follow the signed start of Deer Creek Trail (Forest Trail 45). The trail works

Shake Canyon

Cactus Ridge

Bars Canyon

Deer Creek

Bar T Bar
Ranch

87

× 7400'

Deer Creek

Deer Creek Trail

South Fork Deer Creek

Tr 46

Tr 45

FR 492

188

Tr 47

87

△ Chilson Camp

Maple Spg.

7100 Mount
Peeley

FR
201

End

× Pine Butte
6400

One Mile

NORTH

its way north about .5 mile through desert grassland and drops into Deer Creek. It then follows the creek west through riparian growth of cottonwood and sycamore trees (the stream flows most of the year). After about two miles, the trail passes the creek's confluence with Bars Canyon. The trail becomes narrower and rougher, climbing along the south wall of the canyon. Over the next three or four miles the trail climbs steadily, finally entering a fine stand of ponderosa pine just before reaching the site of Chilson Camp (McGowan Camp on the wilderness map). This area of open meadows offers a number of possible campsites. There is normally water in the creek except during long dry periods.

Forest Trail 45 continues up the creek a short distance then climbs steeply out to the south, reaching the Mount Peeley road (Forest Road 201) at its end. It is possible to hike up the Divide Trail (Forest Trail 23) and explore the interesting country around Mount Peeley. It is also easy to hike cross-country up Mount Peeley from the north.

You can return to your car via Deer Creek or else return on Forest Trail 46 via the South Fork of Deer Creek.

Forest Trail 47 follows an especially scenic route. To do this, walk east from the end of Forest Trail 45 on the Mount Peeley road about two miles. Because the road is long and rough there is little traffic. Maple Spring, located just north of the road about a mile east of the Deer Creek Trail, is unsigned but may be a reliable water source. Except near the start where it passes through an old burn, the road stays on north-facing slopes shaded by fine stands of ponderosa pine and Douglas fir. About two miles from the Deer Creek Trail (Forest Trail 45), the road swings abruptly south out of the forest, and at this point Forest Trail 47 forks left (northeast).

The trail starts as a jeep trail which is closed after a short distance, and continues through tall pines, working its way northwest down the complex ridge system. About three miles from the Mount Peeley road, the trees finally give way to chaparral. The foot trail veers right from the old jeep trail and climbs over a small hill, then drops rapidly off the ridge to end at the trailhead. It is a pleasant two-mile walk down the road to the fork near the highway.— *Bruce Grubbs* □

HIKE 58 *BARNHARDT-SHAKE TREE*

General description: Two- or three-day loop hike in the Mazatzal Wilderness Area.
General location: About 18 miles southwest of Payson.
Maps: Mazatzal Peak 7.5-minute; USFS Mazatzal Wilderness map.
Difficulty: Moderate.
Length: About fifteen miles.
Elevation: 4,200 to 6,000 feet.
Water availability: At the trailhead, Chilson Spring, and Y Bar Tanks.
Special attractions: A fine sampler of the rugged terrain along the Mazatzal crest.
Best season: April through November.

For more information: Payson Ranger District, P.O. Box 100, Payson, AZ 85541; (520) 474-7900.
Permit: None.

The hike: From Arizona 87, turn west onto the dirt Barnhardt Road, which is located about three miles north of the junction with Arizona 188. Drive about 5.5 miles to the end of the road. There are three trails which start here: the Barnhardt Trail, the Shake Tree Trail, and the Rock Creek Trail.

Using the Barnhardt and Shake Tree trails, hikers can tackle a classic loop trip around Mazatzal Peak, the spectacular high point of the range. While most of the trails in the Mazatzals are rough and difficult to follow, these two trails were rebuilt by the Forest Service in the late 1960s and have been maintained since. They provide a good introduction to the characteristics of the range.

From the trailhead, follow the signed Barnhardt Trail as it climbs up into Barnhardt Canyon. There are good views of the permanent stream in Barnhardt as the canyon narrows. A series of switchbacks lead around the head of a side canyon; then the trail swings around a point into the upper basin of the Barnhardt drainage. It is worthwhile to walk out on this point; there are excellent views of upper Barnhardt Canyon and the precipitous east slopes of the range. The trail continues through heavy brush, the result of an old fire, past the signed turnoff to Castersen Seep (unreliable) and Sandy Saddle. It passes through some surviving stands of ponderosa pine before reaching Barnhardt Saddle and the junction with the Divide Trail at the head of the canyon.

The Mazatzal Mountains are heavily scarred by old and not-so-old wildfires. In much of Arizona's ponderosa pine country (areas lying at 6,500 feet or higher), ponderosa pine destroyed by fire are eventually replaced by new ponderosa pine. Lower, drier areas like the Mazatzals are not so favorable for ponderosa pine, however, and the burned forest is usually replaced by dense thickets of manzanita and scrub oak. One explanation for this difference is that mature pines are much more tolerant of heat and drought than pine seedlings and so can survive a climate which has become too dry now for seedlings to grow.

From Barnhardt Saddle, you can turn south (left) and start on the Divide Trail, but many hikers take at least half a day to climb up Barnhardt Canyon and so may wish to camp first. Follow the Divide Trail to the right (northeast) about a mile to reach Chilson Camp, which offers numerous fine campsites in scattered pinyon-juniper, superb sunset views of the west face of Mazatzal Peak, and reliable water. (If the pipe is not running at the camp, you may have to follow it up the hill, above the Divide Trail, and do some spring maintenance). Chilson Camp has been used as a line camp by ranchers for many years, and the recent cleanup by the Forest Service has made it a pleasant place for hikers as well.

To continue the loop around Mazatzal Peak, either retrace your steps to Barnhardt Saddle and take the Divide Trail south or take the trail south from Chilson Camp past Brodie Seep. In either case, you will traverse below the west face of Mazatzal Peak to the Windsor Spring saddle, at the junction with the Shake Tree Trail. (Windsor Spring is not reliable.) The Shake Tree Trail descends rapidly into Y Bar Basin where there is reliable water at Y Bar Tanks (unmarked—see Mazatzal Peak quad), then climbs northwest to

Shake Tree Saddle between Cactus Ridge and Mazatzal Peak. You can climb Mazatzal Peak via its southeast ridge from this saddle. From the saddle, the trail descends through a dense ponderosa forest and emerges on dry grassy slopes above Shake Tree Canyon, gradually descending to the Barnhardt trailhead.

Once the hangout of the Apache Indians, the Mazatzals have seen some mining activity but have been mainly used for grazing. These mountains have a reputation for rugged terrain which can quickly be verified by a short venture into one of the many canyons. Even today the long, rough trails seem to discourage most backpackers and only the Mazatzal Peak area is popular.— *Bruce Grubbs* □

HIKE 59 *WILLOW SPRING-RED HILLS*

General description: A five-to seven-day loop hike in the Mazatzal Wilderness Area.

General location: Twenty-five miles southeast of Payson.

Maps: Chalk Mountain 7.5-minute, Table Mountain 7.5- minute, Cypress Butte 7.5-minute, Wet Bottom Mesa 7.5-minute, North Peak 7.5-minute USGS quads; USFS Mazatzal Wilderness map.

Difficulty: Difficult (rough, faint trails).

Length: About forty-one miles.

Elevation: 2,100 to 6,700 feet.

Special attractions: Varied life zones, from Sonoran desert to Transition pine forest; varied terrain, from desert flats to rocky escarpments and deep canyons.

Water availability: See description.

Best season: Spring and fall.

For more information: Payson Ranger District, P.O. Box 100, Payson, AZ 85541; (520) 474-7900.

Permit: None.

The hike: These trails are accessible from the Sheep Bridge Trailhead on the Verde River, one of the more remote trailheads in central Arizona. It can be approached two ways. From Carefree, north of Phoenix, take the Cave Creek Road (Forest Road 24) north approximately thirty miles to the Tangle Creek Road (Forest Road 269). Turn east (right) and drive about ten miles to the Sheep Bridge Trailhead at the end of the road. This route is normally passable except during or after a major winter storm.

You can also reach the Tangle Creek Road via the Bloody Basin Road, by exiting I-17 about two miles south of Cordes Junction (80 miles north of Phoenix), and going east about thirty miles (during which the road becomes Forest Road 269 at the National Forest boundary). This road may be impassable after heavy rain or snow, especially at the Agua Fria River crossing about 5 miles from the freeway.

Despite the long drive, Sheep Bridge is a popular spot. The original footbridge was built by sheepherders to get their animals across the Verde for the long drive north to the highcountry west of Payson. Each year the sheep were moved from their low winter pastures to higher summer pastures and back. The current bridge was constructed by the Forest Service.

The loop trip described here samples some of the incredible variety of the Mazatzal country. Once across the river at the east end of Sheep Bridge, take the signed Willow Spring Trail east through the Sonoran desert foothills. The trail winds through stands of saguaro and cholla cactus and ascends gradually the first several miles. About three miles from Sheep Bridge, it passes close to Horse Creek, easily identified by its tall cottonwood trees, where there is seasonal water. Three miles farther, the trail begins to climb steeply up to Willow Spring Basin (Willow Spring should be reliable) and from there even more steeply to Mountain Spring. Along the way, hikers pass from the saguaro-dominated Sonoran desert to high desert grassland and then to pinyon-juniper woodland. Mountain Spring should be reliable. Both Willow Spring and Mountain Spring are fine campsites.

The old sheep bridge spanning the Verde River was used for many years to move sheep from the desert lowlands to the highcountry. Stewart Aitchison

The trail climbs over a ridge above Mountain Spring, then works its way northeast along a ridge system toward Midnight Mesa, passing Lost Spring (not shown on the USGS map). It swings around the east end of Midnight Mesa, offering fine views of the rugged Maverick Basin area, then descends through stands of Arizona cypress to cross an arm of Wet Bottom Creek. There will be water here in wet years. In dry years, however, you may have to carry water for camp or else continue north on the Red Hills cutoff trail and camp at the Wet Bottom Creek crossing, which should have water in winter and spring. As its name implies, this trail is a shortcut to the Red Hills Trail, and it leaves the Willow Spring Trail just northeast of Midnight Mesa.

The Willow Spring Trail continues northeast from the creek crossing, climbing steeply (again) onto a pine-covered ridge above Maverick Basin, the head of Deadman Creek. It passes through a saddle before contouring north to end at the Divide Trail. There is an unsigned remnant of an old trail shown on the map at the saddle. This is the old Divide Trail. The new Divide Trail junction is just off the edge of the Cypress Butte quad, on the North Peak map.

Now follow the Divide Trail north to The Park, the head of Wet Bottom Creek, which drains most of the northwestern Mazatzals. Here is the junction with the North Peak Trail, a steep but scenic route down the north side of North Peak. The Divide Trail now swings west around a canyon head (where there is seasonal water) and then north over the gentle slopes of Knob Mountain, the high point of the trip at about 6,700 feet. The trail shown on the Cypress Butte quad going west across Knob Mountain is virtually nonexistent, although the route can be followed cross-country.

Continue north on the Divide Trail a mile to the signed junction with the Red Hills Trail, shown on the wilderness map but not the USGS map. Although it is shorter to take the cross-country route across Knob Mountain, this first part of the Red Hills Trail makes going out of your way worthwhile. The Red

The highest point in the Mazatzal Wilderness is Mazatzal Peak at 7,888 feet. The mountain is composed of quartzite, a metamorphosed sandstone, formed nearly two billion years ago. Bruce Grubbs

Hills trail descends the ridge as shown on the topo for a short distance but then turns abruptly west (don't take the old trail down the ridge!) and descends into the head of Boardinghouse Canyon. This area is heavily forested with ponderosa pines and offers a number of nice campsites with water during the cool season.

After about a mile, the trail climbs up another drainage to the northwest side of Knob Mountain and passes the junction with the Wet Bottom Trail. It turns south and drops steeply into the Fuller Seep basin. The seep seems to be reliable and there is good camping in this scenic basin. From here the trail climbs over a ridge, past the junction with the Red Hills cutoff trail, and then works its way down to Wet Bottom Creek. This section of the trail is fainter and may require use of the wilderness map in conjunction with the Cypress Butte quad.

Across the creek, the trail climbs steeply to the top of a cypress-covered ridge, then wanders in a half-circle to the north across the mesa top. The trail is faint and it will be necessary to carefully watch for cairns. You do NOT want to lose the trail. Cross-country hiking in this area is rough and slow.

About 2.5 miles from Wet Bottom Creek, the trail reaches a saddle and turns abruptly west, descending into a drainage (one of the many arms of Wet Bottom Creek). There is camping and seasonal water where the trail crosses the drainage and climbs out to the south. Once on top of the mesa, it swings around to the northwest, then descends to a saddle and drops steeply to an obvious mine in the canyon to the southwest. At the mouth of the canyon, you have abruptly re-entered the land of giant saguaros. The trail continues about two miles south over rolling hills, paralleling a drainage, past the turnoff to Dutchman Grave Spring (which should be reliable). The trail turns west, crosses the drainage, and climbs over a low ridge. On the far side it swings onto HK Mesa and follows the top of the mesa southwest, paralleling the lush drainage of Sycamore Creek, a permanent source of water. At the end of the mesa, Sheep Bridge will be in sight, only a mile away.—*Bruce Grubbs*

HIKE 60 *MOUNT BALDY*

General description: A round-trip day hike or longer into the Mount Baldy Wilderness Area.
General location: Fifteen miles southwest of Springerville.
Maps: Mt. Baldy 7.5-minute USGS quad; USFS Mount Baldy Wilderness map.
Difficulty: Moderate.
Length: Seven miles one way.
Elevation: 9,200 to 11,400 feet.
Special attractions: Views of the White Mountains, alpine environment.
Water availability: West Fork of the Little Colorado River, occasional small side streams.
Best season: Summer through fall.
For more information: Springerville Ranger District, P.O. Box 760, Springerville, AZ 86938; (520) 333-4301; White Mountain Apache Enterprise, Fort Apache Indian Reservation, P.O. Box 218, Whiteriver, AZ 85941; (520) 338-4385.
Permit: None for Forest Service land, but the summit is closed (see description below).

The hike: Begin this popular hike by taking Forest Road 87 out of Greer about six miles to its junction with Forest Road 113. Turn left and drive about two miles to Sheeps Crossing on the west fork of the Little Colorado River. Just before the crossing, turn right onto a spur road that leads one-half mile to the trailhead. The signed trailhead is located here.

The trail begins along the right bank of the West Fork of the Little Colorado River and climbs through wonderful blue spruce forest and alpine meadows where in summer aster, fleabane, penstemon, cinquefoil, and iris bloom. There is evidence of past glacial activity—glacial erratics, large boulders deposited by ice, lie along the canyon floor.

West Fork contains brook, rainbow, and cutthroat trout but the trail is only close to the stream near the trailhead. About three miles from the trailhead, the trail crosses a tributary to West Fork. In another 2 miles it reaches the ridge leading to Baldy Peak. Then a mile from the peak, the East Fork Trail joins your route. Note that the actual high point or "summit" is actually an unnamed point along the ridge.

As you near the Baldy Peak, you are treated to spectacular vistas of the White Mountain region. Within .3 mile from the top, you reach the Apache Reservation boundary. The Apaches have closed the last section of trail to Baldy Peak, so this boundary must serve as the turnaround point for most hikers. You might be able to secure a permit by writing to the Apaches at the address above. The summit is closed to protect spiritual values. Please respect the closure and end your hike at the reservation boundary.—*Stewart Aitchison* □

HIKE 60   *MOUNT BALDY*

NORTH

One Mile

FR 87
To Greer

FR 113

Sheep Crossing
Campground

9220'

NATIONAL
FOREST

West Fork Little Colorado River

River

East Fork Little Colorado

Mount Baldy
11403

APACHE RESERVATION

HIKE 61 *ESCUDILLA MOUNTAIN*

General description: A round-trip day hike into the Escudilla Wilderness Area.

General location: Eight miles north of Alpine.

Maps: Nutrioso 7.5-minute or Escudilla 7.5 minute USGS quad; Apache National Forest map.

Difficulty: Moderate.

Length: Two miles one way.

Elevation: 9,480 to 10,876 feet.

Special attractions: One of the places that inspired Aldo Leopold to write about wilderness.

Water availability: None.

Best season: Summer and fall.

For more information: Alpine Ranger District, P.O. Box 469, Alpine, AZ 85920; (520) 339-4384.

Permit: None.

The hike: This hike features two trailheads, both accessible by driving about six miles north of Alpine on U.S. 666. Turn right onto Forest Road 56. In about 1.5 miles you come to a fork. The left fork, FR 56A, goes a couple of miles and then ends at the Government Trail; the right fork winds a couple of miles along the southern base of the mountain and just before turning away to the south, the Escudilla National Recreation Trail begins. The trailheads may not be signed.

Both trails take you through stands of virgin pine, fir, and spruce to the viewpoint at the lookout, your turnaround point. The Escudilla National Recreation Trail is slightly less steep.

Escudilla Mountain received a little notoriety in conservationist Aldo Leopold's classic work *A Sand County Almanac* as the location where one of the last grizzly bears in Arizona was killed. Today black bear, wild turkeys,

Escudilla
Mountain

×10876'

FR 56A

9280'

Profanity
Ridge

FR 56

Tool Box Draw

9600'

One Mile

NORTH

666

Alpine

HIKE 62 *BEAR WALLOW*

General description: A long, round-trip day hike into the Bear Wallow Wilderness Area.

General location: Seven miles southwest of Hannagan Meadow.

Maps: Hoodoo Knob 7.5-minute, Maverick SW 7.5-minute USGS quads; Apache National Forest map.

Difficulty: Moderate.

Length: Up to 7.6 miles one way.

Elevation: 6,700 to 8,700 feet.

Special attractions: Running stream in dense coniferous forest.

Water availability: Stream is permanent.

Best season: Summer and fall.

For more information: Alpine Ranger District, P.O. Box 469, Alpine, AZ 85920; (520) 339-4384.

Permit: None.

The hike: From Hannagan Meadow, drive about six miles south on U.S. 666. Turn right onto Forest Road 25; drive about four miles to the junction with Forest Road 25B and park. Your trail, Forest Trail 63, starts here and heads left (south) as a logging road. The foot trail begins after about eighty yards.

This hike follows the length of the drainage. At mile 2.6, this trail intersects with the Reno Trail (Forest Trail 62), and at mile 7.1 it intersects the Gobbler Point Trail (Forest Trail 59). The Bear Wallow Trail ends abruptly at the San Carlos Indian Reservation boundary, which is marked by a fence and serves as your turnaround point.

The dominant vegetation here is the riparian habitat along the creek with mature ponderosa pine and Gambel oak on the south-facing slopes. The north-facing slopes have mostly spruce and firs. Currently fishing is not allowed in the creek.

Pete Slaughter in 1884 drove cattle into this valley and saw the numerous bear wallows along the creek where the bears came to ward off pesky flies. Black bears still roam the valley, as do elk, mule deer, and mountain lion.—

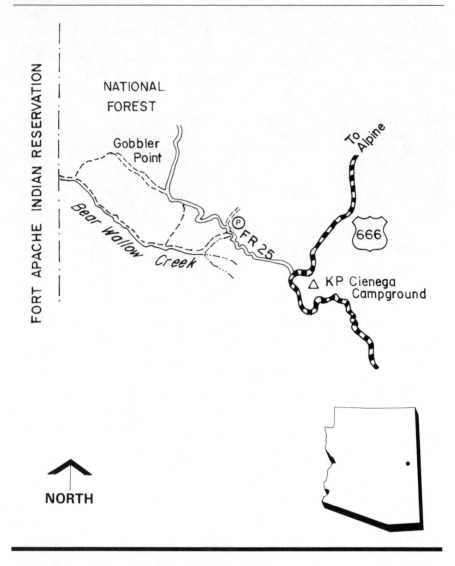

NATIONAL FOREST

Gobbler Point

FORT APACHE INDIAN RESERVATION

Bear Wallow Creek

P FR 25

To Alpine

666

△ KP Cienega Campground

NORTH

HIKE 63 *BEAR VALLEY*

General description: A round-trip backpack into the Blue Range Primitive Area.

General location: Thirty miles south of Alpine.

Maps: Dutch Blue Creek 7.5-minute USGS quad; Alma Mesa 7.5-minute USGS quad; Apache National Forest map.

Difficulty: Difficult, trail obscured by cattle paths.

Length: About ten miles one way.

Elevation: 4,800 to 6,900 feet.

Special attractions: Great views of the southern Blue Range and beyond.

Water availability: Landron Springs and Little Blue Spring are reliable; Auger Tank is questionable.

Best season: Spring through fall, although summer can be quite hot.

For more information: Clifton Ranger District, Box 698, Clifton, AZ 85533; (520) 865-2432.

Permit: None.

The hike: The Bear Valley trail is a scenic route with an abundance of spectacular views of the southern portion of the Blue Range and beyond. To reach the trailhead, drive four miles east of Alpine on U.S. 180 and turn south onto Forest Road 281 (also called the Blue River Road). Drive about 30 miles to its southern dead end at a cabin, barn, and corral known as the Smith Place. The last two miles of road include several river crossings which may be impassable during high

Mule deer are common residents of Arizona highcountry. Their large ears are always tuned for danger. Deer in the low desert areas tend to be Sonoran white-tailed deer. Stewart Aitchison

water. Remember that discretion is the better part of valor, especially in a remote area such as this.

The signed Blue River Trail (Forest Trail 101) begins at the Smith Place and follows the river downstream. After hiking about three miles, you intersect the Bear Valley Trail (Forest Trail 55) at the mouth of the Ladron Springs drainage. A trail sign is maintained on a large cottonwood there.

The Bear Valley Trail starts out on the north side of the Landron Springs drainage and passes several small waterfalls. The trail crosses the drainage twice before arriving at Landron Springs, a powerful and constant spring emerging near the base of a large walnut tree. The spring creates a virtual oasis in an otherwise dry setting.

The trail crosses an open area above the springs, contours along conglomerate ash tuff bedrock, and then descends to an old corral in Sycamore Canyon. The trail crosses the canyon going beneath a lone mature sycamore tree, then climbs a gentle slope through mesquite and bedrock to a saddle. The trail crosses the saddle to the east and switchbacks up the ridge, eventually contouring to the north through some rock bluffs. There are exceptional views along this portion of trail.

The route continues northward over a saddle and then descends to cross Auger Canyon at Auger Tank. Usually there is water here, but you may need to rattle the pipe to get it flowing. Cross directly over the dam and then the low point of Auger Mesa. The trail continues across the south fork of Auger Creek and then heads up the north slope of Government Mesa. The ascent is steep and rocky. The top of the mesa has juniper, cactus, and bear grass.

The trail heads east along the ridgeline of Government Mesa and then makes another ascent to Juniper Flats. Finally it follows a drainage down into Bear Valley, where it meets the Little Blue Trail (Forest Trail 41).

Deep in the Blue Range Primitive Area, long and difficult access routes have kept out all but the most dedicated hikers. For those of you looking for solitude, this is the place. Bruce Grubbs

Follow the Little Blue Trail right, past an old cabin to a corral, the turnaround point of the hike. There is often water in the drainage below the cabin. If not, there is dependable water .75 mile farther down-trail in Little Blue Canyon.

Bear Valley was farmed at the turn of the century, and there are remains of an old wagon and a few outbuildings scattered throughout the valley.— *Apache National Forest* □

HIKE 64 *BEAR MOUNTAIN*

General description: A two-day loop hike in the Blue Range Primitive Area.
General location: Twenty-five miles south of Alpine.
Maps: Bear Mountain 7.5-minute or Blue 7.5-minute USGS quad; Apache-Sitgreaves National Forest map.
Difficulty: Moderate.
Length: About fifteen miles.
Elevation: 5,700 to 7,800 feet.
Special attractions: High, cool pine-and-fir forest.
Water availability: Lower Lanphier Canyon, Cashier Spring, Maple Spring.
Best season: May through November.
For more information: Alpine Ranger District, P.O. Box 469, Alpine, AZ 85920; (520) 339-4384.
Permit: None.

The hike: From Alpine, drive east a couple of miles on U.S. 180 and turn south on Forest Road 281. Stay on this road past the junction with Forest Road 232 to the Forest Service's Blue Administrative Site. The Largo Creek-Lanphier Creek Trailhead is signed.

Most of the Blue Range Primitive Area is seldom-visited by hikers and offers a taste of backpacking far from the crowds that haunt other areas. The Blue fully deserves but has never attained congressional protection as a Wilderness Area.

Many of the trails in the Blue Range are faint because of disuse and require some care to follow. The topographic map is a must! From the trailhead, take Forest Trail 51 across the Blue River (please respect the right of way through private land) and on up Lanphier Canyon. After about a mile, Trail 51, your return route, branches off to the right—stay on the Lanphier Trail 5 2. There is normally running water in the first several miles of Lanphier Creek as the trail ascends through fine stands of ponderosa pine. About three miles from the Blue River, the trail leaves the creek for more than a mile. There is limited camping where the trail meets the creek again.

Cashier Spring is probably reliable and is the last likely water source until the trail descends to Maple Spring in Largo Creek on the return. After wet winters, most of these drainages will be running with water, but in dry autumns the water situation can be more serious.

Above Cashier Spring the trail ends at a signed junction. Take Forest Trail 55 right to Campbell Flat. This section of trail wanders through open stands of ponderosa pine and offers numerous campsites, all without water. At Campbell Flat the trail reaches the Mogollon Rim. Turn west at the signed junction onto Forest Trail 54.

This trail wanders west along the hilly rim for several miles, passing through a large burn and eventually reaching a junction with the signed Largo Canyon Trail (Forest Trail 51) at a saddle just below Bear Mountain. It is an easy side trip up to Bear Mountain Lookout, which is manned during the summer fire season.

The Largo Canyon Trail descends into the upper reaches of the creek, where there is seasonal water and several campsites. The signed Telephone Ridge Trail (Forest Trail 42) joins your route, and there should be water at Maple

Spring or Dutch Oven Spring and limited camping in this stretch of the canyon. The trail follows Largo Creek to within a mile of the Blue River, then climbs over the ridge to the northeast and descends to the Lanphier Trail. Turn left and retrace your earlier steps about a mile to the trailhead.—*Bruce Grubbs* □

HIKE 65 *ALGONQUIN TRAIL*

General description: A long, round-trip day hike or leisurely two-day round-trip hike in the Castle Creek Wilderness Area.
General location: Four miles south of Crown King.
Maps: Crown King 7.5-minute USGS quad; Prescott National Forest map.
Difficulty: Moderate.
Length: About four miles one way.
Elevation: 6,850 to 4,600 feet.
Special attractions: Rugged canyons, historic mining areas.
Water availability: Seasonal in Poland Creek and Horsethief Creek.
Best season: April through November.
For more information: Bradshaw Ranger District, 2230 E. Hwy 69, Prescott, AZ 86301; (520) 445-7253.
Permit: None.

The hike: From Interstate 17, take the Bumblebee Exit north of Black Canyon City and drive approximately thirty miles on Forest Road 259 to the old mining town of Crown King (now a summer-home community). Continue south on FR 259 for .5 mile and go south (left) on Forest Road 52 another 2.5 miles to the signed trailhead on the east (left) for Trail 225. This trail is no t shown on the topo map.

The trail starts in a forested flat on the broad ridgetop, then traverses north along the east slopes of Juniper Ridge. About a mile from the trailhead, it drops onto a ridge and then plunges steeply into Horsethief Canyon through rocky and brushy terrain. At the canyon bottom, your trail joins the signed Horsethief Trail. Turn left (north) on this trail and follow it .25 mile to the site of the old Algonquin Mine, the original reason for these trails. Only a few twisted pieces of rail are visible now near the collapsed mouth of the mine, but the ruins and outlines of several cabins are nearby.

The trail continues north (along a section which was improved as a wagon road when the mine was active) to the Crown King Road. The Horsethief Trail climbs south along scenic Horsethief Canyon to the Horsethief Basin Recreation Area.

There are a number of other trails in this area suitable for dayhikes and overnight backpack trips.—*Bruce Grubbs*

Crown King Road

Hells   Hole

Algonquin Mine

One Mile

NORTH

Juniper Ridge

Algonquin Trail

Horsethief Trail

Horsethief Canyon

To
Crown
King

6400'
Observation
Point

FR 52

Horsethief Road

Horsethief Recreation Trail

FR 52

Horsethief Basin

HIKE 66 *BLACK CANYON*

General description: A round-trip day hike in cool pine forest.
General location: South end of Mingus Mountain.
Maps: Cottonwood 7.5-minute USGS quad; Prescott National Forest map.
Difficulty: Moderate.
Length: About six miles one way.
Elevation: 6,600 to 4,200 feet.
Water availability: Seasonal in Black Canyon.
Special attractions: Cool pine forest, live stream, waterfalls.
Best season: May through November.
For more information: Verde Ranger District, Box 670, Camp Verde, AZ 86322: (520) 567-4121.
Permit: None.
Wilderness status: None.

The hike: Take U.S. 89A to the top of Mingus Mountain, east of Precott, and turn south on Forest Road 104. After about 1.5 miles, turn west (right) on Forest Road 413, the Allen Springs Road. This road is passable to most vehicles as far as the Black Canyon Trail but becomes much rougher beyond that point. A little more than 5 miles from Forest Road 104, watch for the signed trailhead for Black Canyon Trail 114.

The trail follows Gaddes Canyon into the gentle forested valley at the head of Black Canyon. About two miles from the road it veers north out of the creekbed and drops down the slopes north of the canyon, ending after about four miles at Quail Springs and the end of Forest Road 359 (accessible from the Verde Valley). This is your turnaround point.

It is possible to descend Black Canyon below the point where the trail leaves the canyon. This is a very rugged but interesting scramble down ledges and waterfalls. You can then take the trail back to your car.—*Bruce Grubbs*

89A

FR104

Mingus

FR413

Mountain

Quail Spring

Allen Springs Road

Black Canyon Trail

Black Canyon

NORTH

One Mile

HIKE 67 *WOODCHUTE*

General description: A round-trip day hike in the Woodchute Wilderness Area.

General location: North end of Mingus Mountain.

Maps: Muno's Draw 7.5-minute, Hickey Mountain 7.5-minute USGS quad; Prescott National Forest map.

Difficulty: Easy.

Length: Five miles one way to north rim of Woodchute Mountain.

Elevation: 7,000 to 7,700 feet.

Special attractions: Easy hiking, fine views of the Verde Valley, Chino Valley, and Sycamore Canyon.

Water availability: None.

Best season: May through October.

For more information: Verde Ranger District, Box 670, Camp Verde, AZ 86322; (520) 567-4121.

Permit: None.

The hike: Park at the Potato Patch Campground just off U.S. 89A, east of the Mingus Mountain pass. Follow a jeep trai l west, then north out of the campground. Trail 102 leaves the jeep road just north of Powerline Tank and works its way north about four miles through mixed pinyon and ponderosa pine forest to the north rim of Woodchute Mountain. In several places, the trail ascends along ridges which offer views of Chino Valley and the remote Juniper Mountains to the west. The Verde Valley and the Red Rock country near Oak Creek Canyon are also visible.

The north rim of Woodchute Mountain offers expansive views of the Sycamore Canyon Wilderness Area and the red rock country we st of Sedona, as well as of the San Francisco Peaks and the Mogollon Rim. The trail continues down the steep slope to end at F orest Road 318A just off the Perkinsville-Jerome road. Return the way you came—*Bruce Grubbs*

Rim

Woodchute   Mountain

Trail No. 102

Woodchute Tank

Woodchute Trail

Black Hills

89A

NORTH

Powerline
Tank

Potato
Patch
Campground

One Mile

Overview

The southern and western parts of Arizona are part of the Basin and Range geologic province, characterized by somewhat parallel rows of mountain ranges separated by valleys. This is by far the hottest and driest part of the state but is s full of surprises such as hidden springs or relict forest atop high peaks. Except for the highest mountains which are sometimes referred to as sky islands, most hiking should be confined to the fall, winter, and spring.

HIKE 68 *BARFOOT LOOKOUT*

General description: A round-trip dayhike in the Chiricahua Mountains.
General location: Approximately 50 miles southeast of Willcox.
Maps: Chiricahua Mountains (Southern Arizona Hiking Club), Coronado National Forest map.
Difficulty: Easy.
Length: 1.6 miles one way.
Elevation: 8,400 to 8,823 feet.
Special attractions: Panoramic views of north end of the Chiricahuas.
Water availability: At campground in season.
Best season: Summer through fall.
For more information: Douglas Ranger District, Rt. 1, Box 228R, Leslie Canyon Road, Douglas, AZ 85607; (520) 364-3468.
Permit: None.

The hike: From Willcox, drive south on Arizona 186, then turn left (east) on Arizona 181. After three miles turn right (south) on Forest Road 42. This maintained dirt road climbs along north-facing slopes to Onion Pass. Turn right(south) onto Forest Road 42D and continue to Rustler Park Campground. There is water at spigots in the campground when it is open (May through November). The signed trailhead is at the north side of the upper loop of the campground.

After 100 yards, turn right at the signed junction and follow the trail as it diagonals upslope to a saddle on the main ridge . Stay right (east) at this unsigned trail junction. The trail contours along the east slope through a magnificent ponderosa pine forest and then reaches another saddle and signed trail junction. Go right to reach the summit in another .25 mile. The open meadow to the west is Barfoot Park, a natural meadow similar to Rustler Park.—*Bruce Grubbs*

HIKE 69 ECHO CANYON

General description: A round-trip day hike into the Chiricahua National Monument Wilderness Area.
General location: One hundred miles east of Tucson.
Maps: Cochise Head 7.5-minute USGS quad, National Monument brochure.
Difficulty: Moderate
Length: About four round trip miles.
Elevation: 6,200 to 6,900 feet.
Special attractions: Spectacular rock formations.
Water availability: None.
Best season: All year.
For more information: Chiricahua National Monument, Dos Cabezas Star Route, Box 6500, Willcox, AZ 85643; (520) 824-35 60.
Permit: None.

The hike: From the Chiricahua National Monument visitor center parking lot, continue on the scenic drive to the Echo Canyon Parking lot, just before the end of the road at Massai Point. The Echo Canyon Trail starts here, and may be hiked as a loop or used to connect to the Rhyolite Trail.

The trail descends gradually from the viewpoint, and after 0.3 miles meets the Rhyolite Trail coming from the left. Turn right and continue as the trail descends into Echo Park. Here the trail winds between tall rock towers, and you may feel as if you are in the artificial canyons of some large city.

Tall ponderosa and Apache pines shade the cool depths of Echo Canyon, which the trail reaches about 1.2 miles from the parking lot. Turn left at the signed junction with the Rhyolite Trail and follow the trail east along the north slopes of upper Rhyolite Canyon. (A right turn and 1.1 miles of hiking will connect you with the Sarah Deming Trail at its junction with the Rhyolite Trail.) Note the contrast in vegetation between here and the Echo Canyon area. This is due to the southern exposure of this slope, which creates a locally drier climate.

After 0.8 miles, another turn left at another signed junction. The trail climbs gradually back toward Massai Point, and rejoins the Echo Canyon Trail 0.3 miles from the parking lot. Turn right to return to your car.—*Bruce Grubbs*

HIKE 69 *ECHO CANYON*

NORTH

One Mile

181

Echo Canyon

X 6300'

X 6800'
Massai Point

Visitor's
Center

Rhyolite Canyon

HIKE 70 *SILVER PEAK*

General description: A round-trip day hike in the Chiricahua Mountains.
General location: Sixty-four miles northeast of Douglas.
Maps: Portal 7.5-minute USGS, Coronado National Forest (Chiricahua Mountains), Chiricahua Mountains (Southern Arizona Hiking Club).
Difficulty: Moderate.
Length: About 4.6 miles one way.
Elevation: 4,900 to 7,975 feet.
Special attractions: Excellent views of the spectacular Portal area and the Chiricahua Mountains.
Water availability: None.
Best season: Spring through fall.
For more information: Douglas Ranger District, Rt. 1, Box 228R, Leslie Canyon Road, Douglas, AZ 85607; (520) 364-3468 .
Permit: None.

The hike: From Douglas, drive fifty-four miles northeast on US 80, and turn right on the signed turnoff to Portal (Forest Road 42). Continue on the main road to the ranger station, and park at the signed trailhead several hundred yards beyond.

The trail leads to the summit of Silver Peak, which is the high point of the massive mountain directly west. The actual summit is hidden from the parking lot. A few yards up the trail, an unsigned trail goes right to the ranger station; turn left here and start up the slope toward the west. This gentle-appearing slope is deceiving—the trail actually climbs 700 feet to reach the base of the mountain. This would be a good goal for family groups or those short on time, as there are excellent views of the towering cliffs of the Portal area.

Now the trail swings around to the north slopes of the mountain and enters sections of cool pine forest. Final switchbacks lead to the rocky summit and the precariously perched old fire lookout. To the west, the dramatic sweep of the Chiricahua high peaks dominates the horizon. Northeast in the distance are the ranges of New Mexico.—*Bruce Grubbs*

HIKE 71 *MONTE VISTA PEAK*

General description: A round-trip day hike in the Chiricahua Wilderness.
General location: Sixty-five miles north of Douglas.
Maps: Chiricahua Peak 7.5-minute USGS, Coronado National Forest (Chiricahua Mountains), Chiricahua Mountains (Southern Arizona Hiking Club)
Difficulty: Moderate.
Length: 4.9 miles one way.
Elevation: 6,600 to 9,357 feet.
Special attractions: One hundred mile views, forest regrowth after wild fire.
Water availability: Bear Spring near summit.
Best season: Spring through fall.
For more information: Douglas Ranger District, Rt. 1, Box 228R, Leslie Canyon Road, Douglas, AZ 85607; (520) 364-3468.
Permit: None.

The hike: From US 666 34 miles north of Douglas, turn east on the signed Rucker Canyon Road (Forest Road 74). After sixteen miles, turn left (east) at the signed junction and continue on the Rucker Canyon Road. In nine miles, Forest Road 74E goes left at a signed junction. This road dead ends in lower Rucker Canyon. Just before Bathtub Campground, watch for Forest Road 628. Take this road left (north); it ends at the trailhead and Wilderness boundary after two miles. A high clearance vehicle is recommended for this rough side road.

At first the Monte Vista Trail follows the old road, but after the road switchbacks right out of the canyon it becomes a foot path. Starting in pine-oak woodland, the trail switchbacks higher following the North Fork of Rucker Canyon. This forest is a fine example of a mature ponderosa forest with many large trees and minimal undergrowth. The Apache pine is also found here. Distinguishable from ponderosa pine by its longer, lighter-colored needles, it is found only in extreme Southeastern Arizona , Southwestern New Mexico, and Northern Mexico.

At Buckskin Saddle, the trail begins climbing Monte Vista Peak itself, climbing in switchbacks, then traversing the south slopes of the mountain. Contrast the pine forest along this stretch to that seen earlier. Here a forest fire burned most of the trees. Those that did survive had all but their uppermost branches burned off, and these are visible as "flag" trees. Young pines are growing in thick "doghair" stands. Eventually most of these trees will lose the competition for sunlight, and only a tiny minority will grow to maturity.

The trail passes the signed spur trail to Bear Spring, and ends one half mile further at the junction with the Crest Trail. It is an easy walk west to the summit. Unlike most Chiricahua Peaks, the top of Monte Vista Peak is mostly bald, giving one of the best views in the range. A fire tower here is manned by Forest Service personnel during the fire season; ask permission of the lookout before you climb the stairs.—*Bruce Grubbs*

HIKE 72 *RUCKER CANYON*

General description: A round-trip day hike along lower Rucker Canyon.
General location: Sixty-six miles north of Douglas.
Maps: Chiricahua Peak 7.5-minute USGS, Coronado National Forest (Chiricahua Mountains), Chiricahua Mountains (Southern Arizona Hiking Club).
Difficulty: Easy.
Length: 2.8 miles one way.
Elevation: 6,200 to 6,700 feet.
Special attractions: Tall, cool pine forest and running stream.
Water availability: Seasonal in Rucker Canyon.
Best season: Spring through fall.
For more information: Douglas Ranger District, Rt. 1, Box 228R, Leslie Canyon Road, Douglas, AZ 85607; (520) 364-3468.
Permit: None.

The hike: Follow the road directions for Monte Vista Peak, but continue to the end of Forest Road 74E instead of turning left on Forest Road 628.

The Rucker Canyon Trail starts from the east end of the campground, and follows the cool, shaded depths of Rucker Canyon for just under three miles. When it abruptly turns right and switchbacks out of the canyon, leave the trail and continue up the canyon, following the stream. After about .25 mile the canyon swings abruptly left (north) and becomes much rougher.

Here, beside the musical stream, it is easy to imagine that modern man has never existed, and that an Apache warrior may glide into view at any moment. There are tantalizing views of the crags and steep forested slopes of the headwaters of Rucker Canyon.

Although the short cross country walk to this point was easy, it would be wise to gain experience on the many trails before attempting more difficult cross country hiking. Off trail, these mountains are steep, brushy, and rocky.

Rucker Canyon is probably named for Lieutenant Rucker, who led an Army detachment from Fort Bowie at the northern end of the Chiricahuas in the late 1800s. His mission took him to the Mule Mountains in search of Apaches who had fled their reservation, possibly for Mexico. While he and his scout found no trace of the Indians, they did discover traces of copper near their camp in what is now downtown Old Bisbee. The resulting copper strike turned out to be one of the richest and longest worked ore bodies in the world. Unfortunately Rucker didn't share in the financial bonanza.—
Bruce Grubbs

HIKE 72 RUCKER CANYON

HIKE 73 _COCHISE STRONGHOLD_

General description: A round-trip day hike in the Dragoon Mountains.
General location: Thirty-six miles south of Willcox.
Maps: Cochise Stronghold 7.5-minute USGS, Coronado National Forest (Dragoon Mountains) map.
Difficulty: Moderate.
Length: Three miles one way.
Elevation: 4,920 to 5,960 feet.
Special attractions: Rugged granite area.
Water availability: At campground.
Best season: Spring through fall.
For more information: Douglas Ranger District, Rt. 1, Box 228R, Leslie Canyon Road, Douglas, AZ 85607; (520) 364-3468.
Permit: None.

The hike: From Willcox, drive west on I-10, then south on US 666. At Sunsites, about twenty-eight miles from Willcox, turn right (west) on the signed road to Cochise Stronghold. Follow this road to its end at the Forest Service campground.

After leaving the signed trailhead, the path climbs south into upper Stronghold Canyon. About a mile from the campground, a spur trail goes left; stay right. The next half mile of trail works through rugged terrain dotted with granite boulders and cliffs. Finally the trail swings left onto the south slopes of the canyon and contours to the pass at the head of Stronghold Canyon. Retrace your route to return.

Cochise Stronghold is named after Cochise, the famous chief of the Chiricahua Apaches who waged war on the early settlers of southeastern Arizona and northern Sonora. After raids, the band would retreat to this rugged area to evade pursuit.—_Bruce Grubbs_

HIKE 74 MILLER PEAK

General description: A round-trip day hike in the Huachuca Mountains.
General location: Twenty miles south of Sierra Vista.
Maps: Miller Peak 7.5-minute, Montezuma Peak 7.5-minute USGS, Coronado National Forest (Huachuca Mountains) map.
Difficulty: Moderate.
Length: Five miles one way.
Elevation: 6,550 to 9,466 feet.
Special attractions: Scenic ridge, views south into Mexico.
Water availability: None.
Best season: Spring through fall.
For more information: Sierra Vista Ranger District, 5990 S. Hwy 92, Sierra Vista, AZ 85635; (520) 378-0311.
Permit: None.

The hike: Miller Peak is the highest point in the Huachuca Mountains, and it and the rest of this scenic mountain range are the "sierra" from which the city of Sierra Vista derived its name. From Sierra Vista, drive south on Arizona 92 approximately fifteen miles and turn right (south) on the signed road to Coronado National Memorial. Follow the road to Montezuma Pass (the last section is maintained dirt).

The Miller Peak Trail starts up the grassy ridge north of the parking area and climbs across the slope to a saddle, then begins switchbacking up a south facing slope. This section offers fine views of Montezuma Canyon to the south-east. The trail soon reaches the top of the main ridge and follows it north toward Miller Peak. Notice the contrast between the grassy, high desert slope you have just left, and the densely vegetated slopes of Ash Canyon below you. Although the elevations are the same, the growing conditions are radically different due to the amount of sun received.

A more alpine mix of vegetation begins to dominate as the dry, brushy ridge is left behind for the ascent of the peak itself.

Here the trail winds through rough granite terrain before passing the junction with the Huachuca Crest Trail. A few final switchbacks lead to the windswept summit.—*Bruce Grubbs*

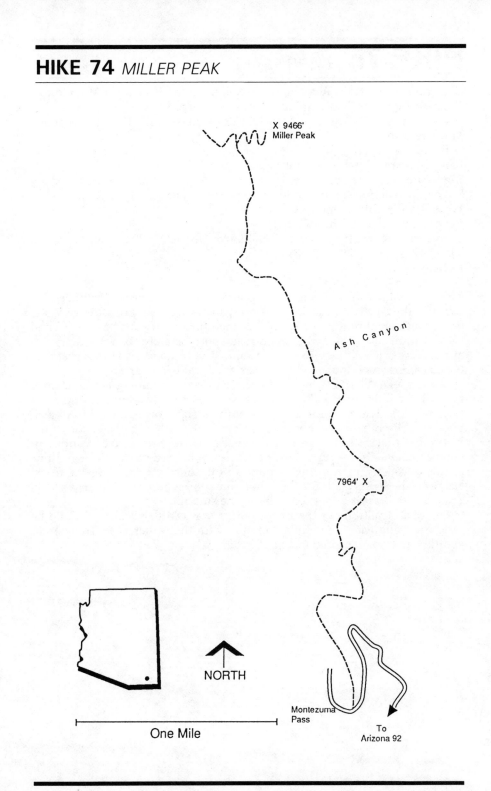

X 9466'
Miller Peak

Ash Canyon

7964' X

NORTH

One Mile

Montezuma
Pass

To
Arizona 92

HIKE 75 *CARR PEAK*

General description: A round-trip day hike in the Huachuca Mountains.
General location: Fourteen miles south of Sierra Vista.
Maps: Miller Peak 7.5-minute USGS, Coronado National Forest (Huachuca Mountains) map.
Difficulty: Moderate.
Length: Approximately 2.5 miles one way.
Elevation: 7,420 to 9,250 feet.
Special attractions: High trailhead, expansive views.
Water availability: None.
Best season: Spring through fall.
For more information: Sierra Vista Ranger District, 5990 S. Hwy 92, Sierra Vista, AZ 85635; (520) 378-0311.
Permit: None.

The hike: Unlike many hikes in the "island" mountain ranges of southeastern Arizona, this one begins from a relatively high trailhead. From Sierra Vista, drive south eight miles on Arizona 92, then turn right (west) on the signed Carr Canyon road. Follow the main road approximately six miles to its end at the second Forest Service campground. The trailhead is at the west side of the campground loop, and there is signed trailhead parking.

The Carr Peak Trail turns southwest and starts climbing a gentle ridge through the old Carr Peak burn. After passing through a surviving stand of tall timber, a signed trail forks left. Continue right, on the main trail, as it begins to climb more steeply toward Carr Peak. Although the shade of the burned forest is sorely missed, the beautiful views are wonderful compensation. On the north side of the peak, the trail passes through thick stands of aspens, then swings around to the south slopes. Here the forest survived the fire. Watch for the signed junction where the Carr Peak Trail branches right. It is about 0.2 miles to the summit.

The main trail follows the ridge south toward Miller Peak and could be used for a one way hike in combination with the Miller Peak Trail. A car shuttle would be required.—*Bruce Grubbs*

To Ramsey Canyon

Comfort
Spring

Canyon

Road

Carr

Old Sawmill
Spring

NORTH

Carr Peak
9225' X

To
Miller Peak

One Mile

HIKE 76 *UPPER RAMSEY CANYON*

General description: A round-trip day hike in the Huachuca Mountains.
General location: 14 miles south of Sierra Vista.
Maps: Miller Peak 7.5-minute USGS, Coronado National Forest (Huachuca Mountains) map.
Difficulty: Easy.
Length: Approximately two miles one way.
Elevation: 7,420 to 6,800 feet.
Special attractions: High trailhead, wildlife area.
Water availability: Seasonally at Comfort Spring.
Best season: Spring through fall.
For more information: Sierra Vista Ranger District, 5990 S. Hwy 92, Sierra Vista, AZ 85635; (520) 378-0311.
Permit: None.

The hike: Follow the road directions for Carr Peak; both hikes share the same trailhead. The trail descends slightly to cross the head of Carr Canyon. To the south, Carr Peak dominates the basin, which was burned by a major fire in the early seventies. About 0.5 miles from the trailhead, Comfort Spring offers seasonal water. The trail now climbs north to reach a saddle, and then descends gradually into Ramsey Canyon. The cool forested mountainside is a relief after the starkness of the Carr Canyon burn.

The trail ends at the bottom of Ramsey Canyon, about two miles from the trailhead. It is easy to explore either up or down the canyon from here. Ramsey Canyon is very popular with birders, as a number of rare species are found here.—*Bruce Grubbs*

HIKE 77 *BETTY'S KITCHEN*

General description: A self-guided loop nature trail located southwest of Mittry Lake and northeast of Laguna Dam along the lower Colorado River.
General location: Fifteen miles northeast of Yuma.
Maps: Laguna Dam 7.5-minute USGS.
Difficulty: Easy.
Length: 0.5 mile.
Elevation: 155 feet.
Special attractions: Outstanding bird-watching area.
Water availability: None.
Best season: September to May.
For more information: Bureau of Land Management, 3150 S. Winsor Avenue, Yuma, AZ 85365; (520) 726-6300.
Permit: None (day-use only, no overnight camping).

Laguna Dam

P

To Mittry Lake

To Yuma
(Ave 7E)

NORTH

One Mile

The hike: From Yuma take US 95 east to Avenue 7E (Laguna Dam Road). Head north for nine miles until the paved road turns to a gravel road. Proceed another 0.5 miles and look for the Betty's Kitchen interpretive sign located on the right side of the road. At the trail's head there is a brochure box with trail guides.—*Bureau of Land Management* □

HIKE 78 *SQUAW LAKE NATURE TRAIL*

General description: A self-guided round-trip nature trail located east of Squaw Lake Recreation Area along the lower Colorado River.

General location: Twenty-three miles north of Yuma.

Maps: Imperial Reservoir 7.5-minute USGS.

Difficulty: Easy.

Length: One mile one way.

Elevation: 200 to 340 feet.

Special attractions: Unique desert area with historical overlooks.

Water availability: Outside the first set of restrooms.

Best season: September to May.

For more information: Bureau of Land Management, 3150 Winsor Avenue, Yuma, AZ 85365; (520) 726-6300.

Permit: None for day hikes (fee for overnight camping).

The hike: From Yuma proceed north over the Fourth Avenue Bridge into California. Take Highway S-24 in Winterhaven, head north for twenty miles, then look for the informational signs on the right side of the road. A nature trail guide is available at the BLM office in Yuma.—*Bureau of Land Management*

HIKE 78 *SQUAW LAKE NATURE TRAIL*

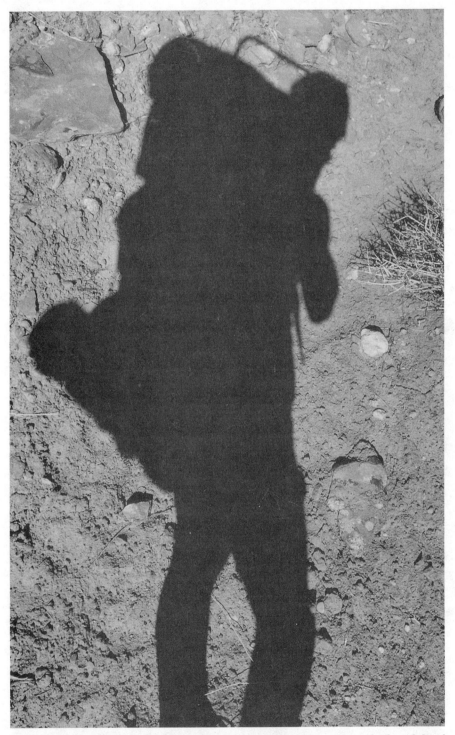

There are many hiking opportunities near Arizona metropolitan areas. Check with local city visitor centers for maps and information about the developing Urban Trail systems. Stewart Aitchison

HIKE 79 *CLARK PEAK*

General description: A round-trip day hike in the Pinaleno Mountains.
General location: Forty miles southwest of Safford.
Maps: Webb Peak 7.5-minute, Blue Jay Peak 7.5-minute USGS, Coronado National Forest (Pinaleno Mountains) map.
Difficulty: Easy.
Length: Four miles one way.
Elevation: 9,000 to 8,500 feet.
Special attractions: Expansive views of southeastern Arizona, close-up views of wildfire effects.
Water availability: None.
Best season: Summer through fall.
For more information: Safford Ranger District, P.O. Box 709, Safford, AZ 85546; (520) 428-4150.
Permit: None.

The hike: Follow the road directions for Ash Creek Falls then continue on the Swift Trail (Forest Road 803) to its end. The Clark Peak Trail is signed and continues along the ridge to the west. The first mile or so of trail descends gently through mature Douglas fir forest, winding around Clark Peak to a sharp saddle and the signed junction with the Nuttall Canyon Trail. Continue on the Clark Peak Trail as it traverses the warmer south slopes toward Taylor Pass.

The alert hiker will notice a few signs of the forest fire that swept through this area, but will probably not be prepared for the scene of utter devastation after crossing the saddle south of Peak 8,790. Continue out onto the slope as the trail gently switchbacks down the grassy meadow.

This burn, which probably happened in the mid-1970's, is an excellent example of a fire occurring under extreme burning conditions. The weather was probably dry for a long period before the fire, and high winds fanned the flames. The result was a highly destructive crown fire, in which the fire literally blew through the treetops and the heat reached such intensity that even the soil was damaged. Listening to the wind whistling erily through the standing snags, it is hard to believe that this was once a cool and beautiful forest, similar to the forest at the trailhead.

Looking closely, one can see the new growth of pine, aspen, and oak which are paving the way for the return of the climax fir forest. On the walk back to the trailhead, the cool depths of the forest seem even more inviting than on the way out.

Experienced hikers may want to continue across Taylor Pass to West Peak and beyond as a long day hike or a backpack trip. The trail drops over a thousand feet to Taylor Pass then climbs steeply up West Peak, and shade is limited most of the way.—*Bruce Grubbs*

174

HIKE 79 *CLARK PEAK*

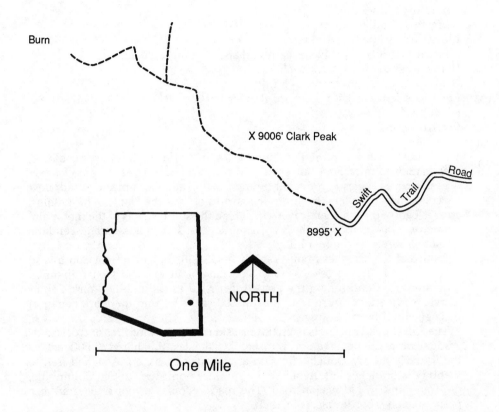

Burn

X 9006' Clark Peak

Swift Trail Road

8995' X

NORTH

One Mile

HIKE 80 *ASH CREEK FALLS*

General description: A round-trip day hike through cool alpine forest.
General location: Thirty-file miles southeast of Safford.
Maps: Webb Peak 7.5-minute USGS, Coronado National Forest (Pinaleno Mountains) map.
Difficulty: Moderate.
Length: 2.5 miles one way.
Elevation: 9,500 to 8,100 feet.
Special attractions: Live stream and spectacular waterfall.
Water availability: Ash Creek.
Best season: Summer through fall.
For more information: Safford Ranger District, P.O. Box 709, Safford, AZ 85546; (520) 428-4150.
Permit: None.

The hike: The trails in the Pinaleno Mountains offer high forested coolness, even in mid-summer. Snow lingers into May and may return as early as October. Access to these hikes is provided by the Swift Trail. This amazing road, now paved for most of its length, climbs the north slopes of the Pinaleno Mountains, crosses Ladybug Pass, then traverses high on the south slopes of the mountain. Numerous trails start from the Swift Trail Road or spur roads, and descend the mountain slopes to the foot hills.

From Safford, drive seven miles south on US 666, then turn right (southwest) onto the Swift Trail (Arizona 366). The pavement ends just past Shannon Campground. Continue on the graded dirt road to Columbine Work Center (Forest Service), then turn right (north) 100 yards beyond the work center at the signed trailhead parking.

The Ash Creek Trail starts from the east side of the parking area and descends gradually into the headwaters of the creek. The elevation here is 9,500 feet, so the forest is mostly Douglas fir with a few quaking aspen. A signed trail to Webb Peak branches left. Avoiding the summer home area at Old Columbine, the trail joins an old wagon road. The road becomes a foot trail again at a pretty meadow bordering Ash Creek.

About 0.5 miles below the meadow, a bypass trail for horses climbs out on the left. Stay right, and you reach Slick Rock, a section where the trail was blasted out of the granite. At the end of this section the stream cascades down steep slabs, and the trail climbs out on the left. Just where the view to the north opens out, Ash Creek Falls can be heard far below the trail, and is visible through breaks in the trees. The fall drops more than 200 feet over a nearly vertical cliff. To the north are visible long expanses of the Mogollon Rim, the White Mountains, and the Mogollon Mountains of New Mexico, as well as the town of Safford and the Gila River Valley 5,000 feet below.—*Bruce Grubbs*

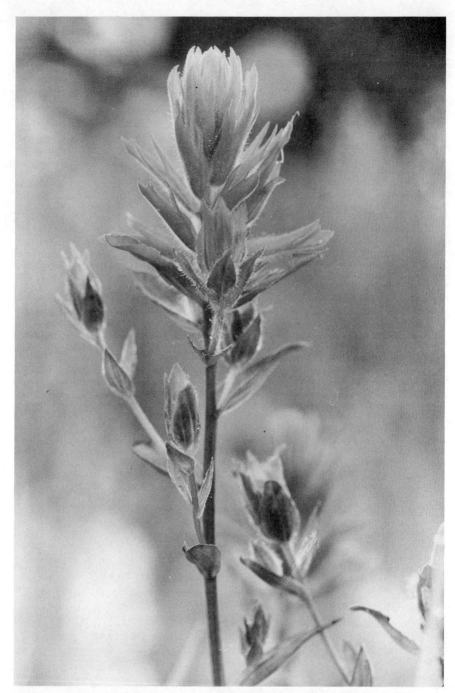

Indian paintbrush is one of the many wildflowers that bloom in the spring in meadows and woodlands. Also known as paintedcups, some species may be red and yellow or just yellow. At high elevations, they may bloom in July or August. Michael S. Sample photo.

Pronghorn antelope are usually seen in small bands on sagebrush plains. Fast runners, these animals may reach speeds of forty mph. Michael S. Sample

HIKE 81 *WEBB PEAK*

General description: A loop day hike to a 10,000 foot peak in the Pinaleno Mountains.
General location: Thirty-five miles southwest of Safford.
Maps: Webb Peak 7.5-minute USGS, Coronado National Forest (Pinaleno Mountains) map.
Difficulty: Easy.
Length: Four miles round trip.
Elevation: 9,500 to 10,030 feet.
Special attractions: Expansive view, cool alpine forest.
Water availability: None.
Best season: Summer through fall.
For more information: Safford Ranger District, P.O. Box 709, Safford, AZ 85546; (520) 428-4150.
Permit: None.

The hike: Follow the road directions given for Ash Creek Falls to reach the same trailhead. Start on the Ash Creek Trail but turn left after about 0.5 miles onto the signed Webb Peak Trail. The trail is actually an old road, probably built during fire-fighting efforts. Meandering through beautiful mountain forest, the trail eventually reaches an old burn and turns south toward the summit. Follow the trail carefully through here as it is easy to lose in the meadows. There are excellent views into the head of Blair Canyon as the trail climbs steeply the last 0.5 mile to the summit. Turn left on the maintained road to walk the last 100 yards to the old fire lookout on the summit.

Next to the Forest Service cabin, a sign marks the start of the return trail to the public corral and trailhead. This trail descends directly down the southeast ridge and reaches the parking lot in less than a mile.—*Bruce Grubbs*

HIKE 82 *LADYBUG PEAK*

General description: A round-trip dayhike to an easily-reached peak in the Pinaleno Mountains.
General Location: Approximately twenty-five miles southwest of Safford.
Maps: Stockton Pass 7.5-minute USGS, Coronado National Forest (Pinaleno Mountains) map.
Difficulty: Easy.
Length: 0.5 miles one way.
Elevation: 8,495 to 8,780 feet.
Special attractions: Easily reached viewpoint, contrasting forest types.
Water availability: None.
Best season: Summer though fall.
For more information: Safford Ranger District, P.O. Box 709, Safford, AZ 85546; (520) 428-4150.
Permit: None.

The hike: Follow the road directions for Ash Creek Falls, stopping at Ladybug Pass where the Swift Trail road first reaches the main crest of the range. The signed trailhead is confused by false trails the trail starts by traversing to the left (north) but switchbacks to the right while the parking area is still in sight. The first section of trail climbs through a mixed forest where Douglas fir and limber pine mingle with ponderosa pine and various oaks. The elevation is high enough that the fir and limber pine find the temperatures cool enough and the moisture supply adequate, yet it is not too cold for the ponderosa.

After a short distance, the trail crosses to the north slope. Here the local climate is slightly cooler and wetter, which is enough to allow the fir forest to dominate. Turn right at the unsigned trail junction to reach the rocky summit. To the west, beyond Ladybug Pass, Heliograph and Plain View Peaks are visible. The highest point, Mount Graham, is hidden.—*Bruce Grubbs*

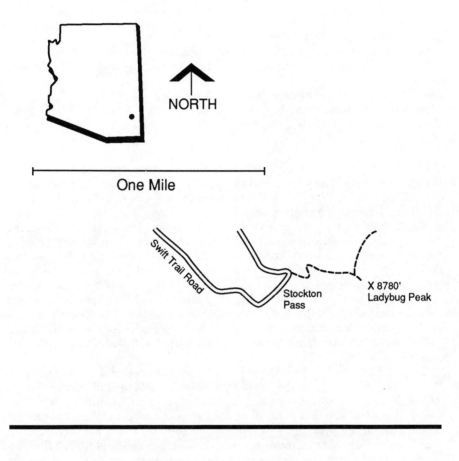

One Mile

Swift Trail Road

Stockton
Pass

X 8780'
Ladybug Peak

NORTH

HIKE 83 *CAVE CANYON TRAIL*

General description: A lesser traveled trail in the Santa Rita Mountains.
General location: Fifty four miles south of Tucson.
Maps: Mt. Wrightson 7.5-minute USGS, Coronado National Forest map, Santa Rita Mountains (Southern Arizona Hiking Club) .
Difficulty: Moderate.
Length: 4.8 miles one way.
Elevation: 6,200 to 9,453 feet.
Special attractions: Superb views, cool pine and fir forest.
Water availability: Seasonally in Cave Creek and Armour, Baldy, and Bellows Springs.
Best season: Spring through fall.
For more information: Nogales Ranger District, 2251 N. Grand Ave., Nogales, AZ 85621; (520) 281-2296.
Permit: None.

The hike: Cave Canyon represents an alternate, less-traveled route to the 9,000 foot crest of the scenic Santa Ritas. This hike may be continued to the summit of Mount Wrightson. There is a fine view point just under halfway for those who wish a shorter walk.

From Arizona 83 four miles north of Sonoita, turn west on the signed Gardner Canyon Road (Forest Road 92). After about seven miles turn right onto the signed road to Cave Canyon (still Forest Road 92). The last two miles of this road will require a high clearance vehicle. The road ends at the Wilderness boundary.

The trail is unsigned at the beginning. Follow the old road up the drainage a few hundred yards. Just before the old mine site, bear left. The old road is badly washed out and then becomes a foot trail which crosses the creek above the mine. After this point, the trail is distinct, and all junctions are signed.

The trail climbs steadily, staying mostly on the north side of the canyon. At Florida Saddle it joins the Crest Trail, which starts up a northwest facing slope. Note the contrast between this tall cool forest and the hotter, drier slope you have just left. The dominant tree is the beautiful Douglas fir, found here at the southern end of its range and also north to Canada. After passing the turnoff to Armour Spring, the Crest trail starts across the east slope of the mountain. Watch for a clearing below the trail where rock outcrops provide an excellent view to the west. This spot is a fine goal for those who wish a shorter hike, or who were unable to drive the last section of road.

The Crest Trail continues north about two miles to Baldy Saddle. Here the Super Trail may be used to reach the summit of Mount Wrightson, another 0.9 miles.—*Bruce Grubbs*

HIKE 83 *CAVE CANYON TRAIL*

Florida Saddle

Cave

View

Trail

Trail

92

Crest

Baldy Saddle

9453' X
Mount
Wrightson

One Mile

NORTH

HIKE 84 *FREMONT SADDLE*

General description: A round-trip day hike in the Superstition Mountains.
General location: Forty miles east of Phoenix.
Maps: Weavers Needle 7.5-minute USGS, Superstition Wilderness USFS map.
Difficulty: Moderate.
Length: Two miles one way.
Elevation: 2,400 to 3,770.
Special attractions: Interesting rock formations, classic view of Weaver's Needle.
Water availability: None.
Best season: Fall through spring.
For more information: Mesa Ranger District, P.O. Box 5800, Mesa, AZ 85201; (602) 379-6446.
Permit: None.

The hike: Follow the directions for Hike 86 (Red Tanks Divide) and park at the end of the Peralta Road. The Peralta Trail starts from the north end of the parking area and climbs to the head of Peralta Canyon at Fremont Saddle, passing rock towers and other strange rock formations. From the saddle, there is a much photographed view of Weavers Needle, a rock spire which dominates the western Superstitions.

Peralta was a Spaniard who supposedly discovered gold in this region and made several trips from Mexico to exploit his find. Fremont Saddle is named for John C. Fremont, head of one of several American survey expeditions to the Far West. His name is on many topographic features in the western US.

Most of the pinnacles along the Peralta Trail are composed of rhyolite, a rock formed by material blown from volcanoes. The yellowish cliffs are tuff, a very weak rock also associated with volcanoes. Unfortunately for those who would make their fortune from lost Spanish gold mines, the geology of the Superstition Mountains is not gold-bearing. It is probable that Peralta's mine was located in the country to the west or north of the Superstitions.—
Bruce Grubbs

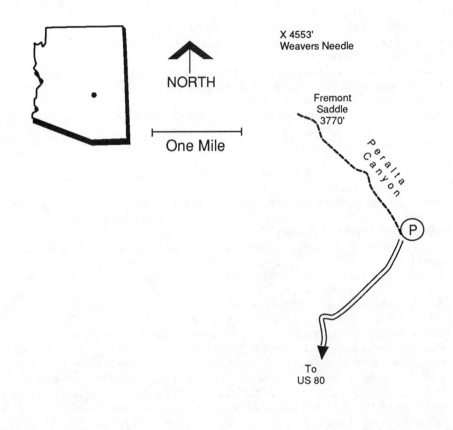

X 4553'
Weavers Needle

NORTH

One Mile

Fremont
Saddle
3770'

Peralta
Canyon

P

To
US 80

HIKE 85 *LOWER LABARGE CANYON*

General description: A round-trip day hike in the Superstition Mountains.
General location: Approximately 35 miles east of Phoenix.
Maps: Goldfield 7.5-minute, Mormon Flat Dam 7.5-minute USGS, Superstition Wilderness USFS.
Difficulty: Easy to moderate.
Length: One to four miles, depending on goal.
Elevation: 1,700 to 2,300 feet.
Special attractions: Dramatic canyon narrows.
Water availability: Seasonally in Labarge Canyon.
Best season: Fall through spring.
For more information: Mesa Ranger District, P.O. Box 5800, Mesa, AZ 85201; (602) 379-6446.
Permit: None.

The hike: From Apache Junction, drive northeast on Arizona 88 approximately fourteen miles to the trailhead at Canyon Lake. A narrow bridge crosses the lake—this is the second bridge since reaching the lake. At the east end of the bridge, note the signed trailhead on the right, and turn left into the trailhead parking.

The Boulder Canyon Trail climbs up the ridge to the south, and the busy road is soon out of sight. After about .7 mile, the main trail turns left and begins switchbacking up the slope. An unsigned spur trail continues south and down into LaBarge Canyon. This junction is an easy goal for those desiring a taste of the wildness of the Superstition Mountains.

Continuing on the main trail, follow it as it climbs along a ridge system with excellent views to the north. About two miles from the trailhead, the trail crosses a saddle and descends to the bottom of LaBarge Canyon. Where the trail crosses the creek bed, leave it and continue cross country upstream past the towering walls of Battleship Mountain. About 1.5 miles from the trail, the canyon walls narrow dramatically; cottonwood trees and pools of water grace the stream. Return the way you came.—*Bruce Grubbs*

HIKE 86 RED TANKS DIVIDE

General description: A three or four-day loop hike in the Superstition Mountains.

General location: Forty miles east of Phoenix.

Maps: Weavers Needle 7.5-minute USGS, Superstition Wilderness USFS.

Difficulty: Difficult

Length: Approximately twenty-one miles.

Elevation: 2,400 to 3,700 feet.

Special Attractions: Rugged, remote desert mountains.

Water availability: Seasonally at Dripping Spring, LaBarge Spring Number 2, Whiskey Spring, Bluff Spring, Crystal Spring, and in Barks Canyon.

Best season: Fall through spring.

For more information: Mesa Ranger District, P.O. Box 5800, Mesa, AZ 85201; (602) 379-6446.

Permit: None.

The hike: From Apache Junction drive southeast on US 60 fourteen miles, then turn left (north) on the signed Peralta Road. Follow this dirt road to its end, approximately 7.5 miles. Several trails leave this popular trailhead; our trip starts on well travelled trails but loops through much less-visited country.

Although this is a desert area with limited water, careful planning around the known water sources will ensure an enjoyable trip. In winter and spring, many of the streams will be running, allowing flexibility in camping. In the fall, water will be more limited.

Start on the signed Dutchmans Trail, then turn right at the signed junction with the Bluff Spring Trail. The Dutchmans Trail continues east, climbing over the low hills. An expansive view of the southern Superstition Mountains opens out ahead, and the trail descends to skirt the northern edge of the broad valley. Miners Needle is visible ahead to the left. Just before the trail swings left up Miners Canyon, turn right onto the Coffee Flat Trail, which climbs through the low saddle to the southeast. The trail works through the low hills of Coffee Flat to Reeds Water (not a reliable water source), then starts up Randolph Canyon. At Dripping Spring, turn left on the Red Tanks Trail. Camping is limited near the spring but is better in Red Tanks Canyon.

About 2.5 miles north of Dripping Spring, the head of Red Tanks Canyon divides, and the trail turns left to ascend the west fork to Red Tanks Divide. This section of the trail is vague and will probably require close work with the topographic map. Northwest of the Divide, the trail descends into LaBarge Canyon. During the cool season, there is usually water in the bare rock drainages here (the "Red Tanks").

The Red Tanks Trail now heads west through dramatic Upper LaBarge Box. There is seasonal water where the trail crosses the creek in the box, and several campsites at the west end. About 0.5 mile west of these campsites, turn left on the Whiskey Spring Trail. Whiskey Spring is usually reliable. At Miners Summit, turn right on the Dutchmans Trail as it descends gently to Bluff Spring. The water is usually reliable and there is camping in the area.

Turn left (west) onto the Bluff Spring Trail, which climbs to the head of Bluff Spring Canyon, then descends left into Bark Canyon. Stay left at the junction with the Terrapin Trail, and remain on the Bluff Springs Trail 2.5 miles to the Peralta trailhead.—*Bruce Grubbs* □

HIKE 86 *RED TANKS DIVIDE*

HIKE 87 REDFIELD CANYON

General Description: A round-trip day hike in the remote Galiuro Mountains.

General Location: Ten miles east of Redington.

Maps: Cherry Spring 7.5-minute USGS, Coronado National Forest (Galiuro Mountains) map.

Difficulty: Moderate.

Length: Two to ten miles.

Elevation: 3,400 to 4,000 feet.

Special Attractions: Scenic riparian areas, canyons, birds, and wildlife.

Water Availability: Seasonally in Redfield Canyon.

Best Season: Fall through spring.

For more information: Bureau of Land Management, 425 E. 4th St., Safford, AZ 85546, (520) 428-4040; The Nature Conservancy, RR 1, Box 1542, Willcox, AZ 85643; Safford Ranger District, P.O. Box 709, Safford, AZ 85546, (520) 428-4150.

Permit: None.

The hike: From San Manuel, drive south on the Redington Road approximately twenty-two miles to an unmarked turnoff going east from Redington. This road parallels the north rim of Redfield Canyon. Alternatively, you may reach this turnoff by driving forty miles north from Benson. The side road is rough and a four-wheel drive is recommended. Do not take any of the right turns until approximately ten miles from Redington, then park on the right overlooking Redfield Canyon.

The old dirt road descends and soon becomes a foot trail, ending at the bottom in one mile. From here, it is possible to explore Redfield Canyon up or downstream, as well as Swamp Springs Canyon. A loop hike may be made by following an overgrown, seldom-used trail out of Redfield Canyon alongside the first major ephemeral drainage from the west, approximately two miles north of Swamp Springs Canyon. This trail returns to the mesa top and a dirt road that leads back to the parking area.

This unique hiking area is partially on public land administered by the Bureau of Land Management and the US Forest Service, and private land owned by The Nature Conservancy. The Forest Service land is part of the Galiuro Wilderness, and the BLM Land is part of the new Redfield Canyon Wilderness. Although the private landowners haven't restricted access to date, they may in the future. Please respect this natural area, and leave everything as you found it.—*Bureau of Land Management*

One Mile

NORTH

Redfield Canyon

GALIURO MOUNTAINS

To Redington

Redfield Canyon

Swamp Springs Canyon

P

HIKE 88 *POACHIE RANGE*

General description: Exploratory hikes in rugged granitic and lava mountains within the Arrastra Mountain Wilderness Area.

General location: Fifty miles northwest of Wickenburg.

Maps: Arrastra Mountain 7.5-minute, Arrastra Mountain NE 7.5-minute, Arrastra Mountain SE 7.5-minute, Palmerita Ranch 7.5- minute, Artillery Peak 15-minute USGS quads.

Difficulty: Easy to difficult (cross-country).

Length: Optional.

Elevation: About 1,400 to 4,807 feet.

Special attractions: Interesting geology, unusual mixture of Mohave Desert, Great Basin, and Sonoran Desert plants; solitude.

Water availability: A few springs shown on topos.

Best season: Fall, winter, spring.

For more information: Bureau of Land Management, Phoenix District Office, 2015 West Deer Valley Road, Phoenix, AZ 850 27; (602) 863-4464.

Permit: None.

The bite of the giant desert centipede is painful but otherwise is not a serious injury. The tip of each of the centipede's forty-two legs is equipped with a sharp claw which may make tiny punctures, but a double pair of jaws under the head do the actual biting. Unless you make a habit of putting your bare hand under rocks or into crevices, you are unlikely to be bitten. Bruce Grubbs

NORTH

Poachie Range

Signal Mt. 2351'

×2000'
×2382'
×2217'
×2598'

8 Miles
To 93

Arrastra Canyon

Big Sandy River

One Mile

The hike: This BLM Wilderness Area does not have any designated trails; however, cross-country travel is fairly easy and adds to hikers' sense of discovery.

One approach is to turn off of Arizona 93 about fifty miles northwest of Wickenburg (mile post 132). Drive south about nine miles and then turn left onto an unsigned but well-graded road. Drive another 3.2 miles and park along the edge of the road. From here hike due south, crossing several washes, and then pick a path of least resistance over the black lava ridges and mesas facing you. You will encounter an old fence at the top of the ridge. Once over the fence, there are many options for hiking. One is to go to the top of Signal

Mountain to the southwest; another is to follow one of the several main washes upstream to narrow granite gorges similiar to the inner gorge of the Grand Canyon.

The desert vegetation consists of such typical Sonoran species as catclaw acacia, ocotillo, saguaro, barrel cactus, beavertail cactus, desert willow, creosote bush, palo verde, brittlebush, and Bigelow nolina. Mixed in with these are Mohave Desert species of yucca, false palo verde, sugar sumac, and desert trumpet. Mormon tea, snakeweed, and juniper are also present, species more typical of the Great Basin Desert.

Several species of cholla are common, including the fuzzy-looking but painful teddy bear jumping cholla. A slight brush against this plant causes a joint or section of stem to break off and stick to you. On top of Signal Mountain are clumps of Christmas cholla, often with bright red fruit.

Common residents of this area include Yuma antelope squirrels which look like chipmunks, mule deer, cactus mouse, white-throated wood rat, pocket mouse, kangaroo rat, black-tailed jackrabbit, and desert cottontail. Feral burros and a few cows also wander the area. On a sunny November day hikers can expect to see the following birds, among others: rock wrens, canyon wrens, cactus wrens, red-tailed hawks, golden eagles, curve-billed thrashers, Gambel's quail, northern flickers, Gila woodpeckers, phainopepla, black-tailed gnatcatchers, and dark-eyed juncoes.

Unfortunately, hikers are also more likely to see pieces of desert tortoise shell than they are to see live tortoises. The desert tortoise population has suffered greatly from livestock overgrazing.—*Stewart Aitchison*

HIKE 89   *SAFFORD-MORENCI TRAIL*

General description: A point-to-point, two-day or longer backpack trip into an historical area.
General location: Twelve miles northeast of Safford.
Maps: Bonita Spring 7.5-minute, Gila Box 7.5-minute, Copperplate Gulch 7.5-minute, Lone Star Mountain 7.5-minute USGS quads.
Difficulty: Moderate.
Length: Fourteen miles one way.
Elevation: 3,700 to 6,000 feet.
Special attractions: Scenic pass, birds, geology, history.
Best season: Spring and fall.
For more information: Safford District Office, Bureau of Land Managment, 425 E. 4th Street, Safford, AZ 85546; (520) 428-4040.
Permit: None.
Wilderness status: BLM Wilderness Study Area.

The hike: To locate the trailhead, drive northeast out of Safford on the San Juan Road. About eight miles down this road, take the left fork heading for Walnut Springs and West Ranch. The trailhead is signed. It is fourteen miles to the end of the trail at the East Trailhead.

By arranging a car shuttle, however, you can avoid having to re-hike the fourteen miles. To do this, drive west out of Morenci on the Eagle Creek Road about five miles and leave a car parked at the East Trailhead.

During wet weather, both roads may be impassable to two-wheel-drive vehicles.

From the Safford-Morenci trailhead, this well-established trail winds through rugged and beautiful canyons with elevations ranging from 3,700 feet to more than 6,000 feet. You will encounter a variety of vegetation types and species, ranging from mesquite and creosote bush at the West Ranch trailhead; to riparian plants like cottonwood, willow, and sycamore along Bonita Creek; to pinyon-juniper and oak in Smith Canyon.

Geological types vary among rhyolite, andesite, and basalt, which together produce majestic rock outcrops and multi-colored formations.

The area provides habitat for mule deer, mountain lion, javelina, rabbit, dove, quail, and a variety of other Sonoran desert species. Bonita Creek is the best area along this hike to see a wide variety of birds, including hawks and eagles.

Cultural features range from prehistoric Indian cliff dwellings in Bonita Creek to remnants of early-day homesteads.

With the advent of the the automobile in the early 1900s, the trail ceased to be used. Recently, however, the Youth Conservation Corps reconditioned the trail for hikers and horseback riders. Please sign the register at the trailhead.

The eerie howl of the coyote is an integral part of the wilderness. Considered a destructive varmint by many ranchers, the coyote nonetheless helps control rabbits, mice, and other rodents. It is also one of the few mammals that has increased its range over the last two centuries in spite of vigorous predator control programs. Stewart Aitchison

HIKE 89 *SAFFORD-MORENCI TRAIL*

East Trailhead 4200'

To Morenci

Bellmeyer Saddle × 6200'

×3700'

High Clearance or 4 WD

West Ranch

West Trail Head × 4800'

San Juan Road To Safford

NORTH One Mile

Bring an ample supply of water for this hike, since streams and springs are scarce. Also purify any water found along the trail before drinking it.

Pioneer farmers and ranchers in the Gila Valley and Bonita Creek area gouged out the Safford-Morenci Trail about 1874. They needed a shorter route to Morenci, Metcalf, and Clifton, where booming mines offered a market for their produce and meat. Also, as the mines developed and the need for wood to burn in the smelters increased, Mexican wood haulers and their pack trains of mules and burros used the trail to haul wood for sale to the copper companies.

Horse rancher Albert Bellmeyer and his foreman rode up this trail from the Morenci side on October 25, 1892. Six years earlier, Geronimo had surrendered, ending for all practical purposes the threat to settlers from hostile Indians. However, renegades had left the San Carlos Reservation for forays as far south as Mexico, 125 miles away. Reports that Indians had been seen on Turtle Mountain prompted Bellmeyer to check on his horse herd grazing on the mountain.

196

What exactly occurred or the sequence of events is conjecture. But evidence at the scene indicates that Bellmeyer and his foreman, a man named Gordonier, were ambushed and had no opportunity to defend themselves. Bellmeyer was shot twice and apparently died instantly, falling from his horse at the notch or "saddle" in the mountain. The two quick shots apparently gave Gordonier a split-second warning, and he wheeled his horse and spurred the frightened animal down the Bonita Creek side of the mountain. But 100 yards down the trail, Gordonier was hit and fell from his horse. The wound was not fatal and the Indians crushed his head with rocks.

When a man named Ben Parks found the bodies and alerted authorities in Morenci, a posse was dispatched to search for the murderers. Other volunteers tied the bodies on mules and took them to Morenci for burial. Before they left, they piled rocks beside the trail where each man had fallen.

The point where the murders occurred was named Bellmeyer Saddle.

The guilty parties were never caught and their identities never known for sure. The infamous Apache Kid and two other renegades, Chato and Natchez, were suspected.

Some of the other people of note who lived near the trail included Toppy Johnson, whose real name was Presley Cantrell. Before coming to Arizona, he had served time in the Santa Fe prison for cattle rustling. Another group of local residents was the Fulchers, who were involved in the illegal horse-trading business. Mother Fulcher committed suicide on Bonita Creek where the trail crosses the creek. Two young cowboys named Putt Golding and Shorty Eaton loaded her remains onto a large mule and transported her via the trail to Morenci. These are just small chapters of the fascinating history associated with this trail.—BLM, Safford District Office

HIKE 90 ARAVAIPA CANYON

General description: A point-to-point or round-trip hike featuring easy walking and splashing through a creek into a colorful canyon amid Sonoran desert vegetation in the Aravaipa Canyon Wilderness Area.

General location: About eleven miles south and ten miles east of Winkleman.

Maps: Brandenburg Mountain 7.5-minute, Booger Canyon 7.5-minute USGS quads.

Difficulty: Easy.

Length: 10.75 miles one way to traverse canyon.

Elevation: 2,600 to 3,100 feet.

Special attractions: Wading through a cool stream while hiking a desert canyon; more than three hundred species of vertebrates including native fish, desert bighorn, mountain lion, and peregrine falcon.

Best season: Spring, summer, or fall. Avoid periods of high water, particularly summertime flash floods.

For more information: Safford District Office, BLM, 425 East 4th St., Safford, AZ 85546, (520) 428-4040 or contact the BLM rangers at Aravaipa East (520) 828-3380 or Aravaipa West (520) 357-7111.

Permit: Obtain from BLM; limited in number and may be difficult to acquire for most weekends during warm months. Permit is required for overnight *and* day use. Length of stay is limited to three days and two nights. There is a fee of $1.50 per person per day. Pets are not permitted in the wilderness and horses are not permitted overnight in the canyon bottom.

The hike: Hikers can enter this ten-mile-long canyon from either side; however, the west entrance is easier to reach and thus more crowded. To reach the west entrance, turn off Arizona 77 onto Aravaipa Road eleven miles south of Winkleman. Take Aravaipa Road past Central Arizona College and proceed for twelve miles along this paved-and-dirt road until you reach the trailhead at a BLM parking lot and ranger station.

The east entrance requires a long drive on gravel roads. Turn off Arizona 70 about eight miles southeast of Ft. Thomas and about thirteen miles northwest of Safford, onto the Klondyke Road. Continue about twenty-five miles and turn right onto the Aravaipa Road, which takes you to Klondyke (about nine miles from the junction), location of the BLM Ranger Station for the east entrance. Continue on for ten miles through five stream crossings to reach the trailhead parking area. There is no trail as such; walking is simply *in* the shallow stream.

Aravaipa Canyon is unusual in that a permanent stream courses through its desert bottom. Sycamore, ash, cottonwood, and willow trees thrive along the creek. The abundance and diversity of wildlife is one of the many charms of this desert canyon. Eleven species of fish swim in the creek; more than fifty species of amphibians and reptiles are known to inhabit the area. Nearly fifty species of mammals have also been recorded here, from desert shrews

All birds have keen eyesight, but turkey vultures are one of the few with a good sense of smell, After a hearty meal of carrion, vultures may have considerable difficulty taking off, but once in the air they search out rising thermals on which to soar effortlessly. From a distance, vultures can be distinguished from hawks by the way they hold their wings—hawks tend to hold their wings flat while gliding; vultures hold their wings at a slight angle or dihedral.
Stewart Aitchison

198

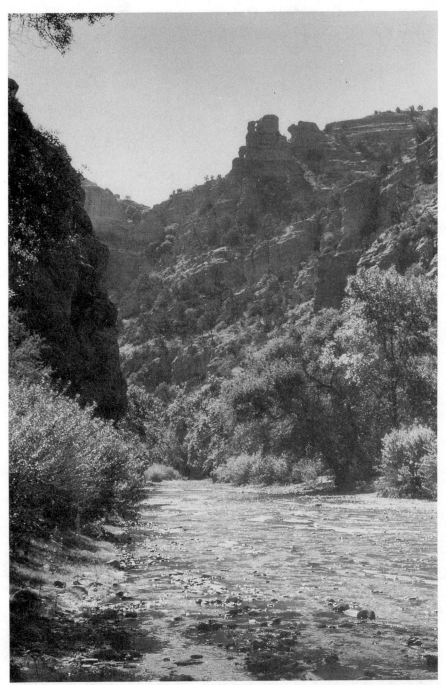

By 1900, overgrazing by livestock and a slight change in the Southwest's rainfall pattern had turned many previously permanent desert streams into intermittent arroyos. The construction of dams on other rivers flooded canyons upstream and dried up the flood plains below the dams. Aravaipa Creek supports one of the last relatively intact desert riparian ecosystems and is a remarkable example of the diversity of desert life. Bruce Grubbs

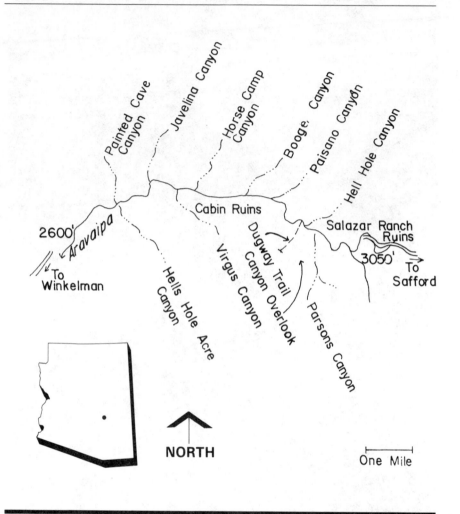

Painted Cave Canyon

Javelina Canyon

Horse Camp Canyon

Booge. Canyon

Paisano Canyon

Hell Hole Canyon

Cabin Ruins

2600'

Aravaipa

To Winkelman

Hells Hole Acre Canyon

Virgus Canyon

Dugway Trail Canyon Overlook

Salazar Ranch Ruins

3050'

To Safford

Parsons Canyon

NORTH

One Mile

to black bear. And, of course, the canyon is a birder's paradise with approximately two hundred species, including rare visits by the endangered peregrine falcon and Mexican species like rose-throated becards.

Evidence of prehistoric people is scattered throughout the Aravaipa region. Turkey Creek Canyon was a primary migration route of Indians, who lived and farmed near Aravaipa Creek.

Pioneers also tried to tame the canyon. Near the mouth of Horse Camp Canyon are the ruins of an unfinished cabin started about 1900. At Hell Hole Canyon is the original homestead of the Salazar family. The cave behind the remnants of the house was also once inhabited by settlers.

If time or energy is short, easy day hikes of two miles one way from either entrance will take you into scenic portions of the canyon.—*Tom Bean* □

HIKE 91 CAMPAIGN-PINE CREEK LOOP

General description: A three- or four-day loop hike in the Superstition Wilderness Area.

General location: Twenty miles northwest of Globe.

Maps: Pinyon Mountain 7.5-minute, Two Bar Mountain 7.5-minute, Haunted Canyon 7.5-minute, Iron Mountain 7.5-minute US GS quads; USFS Superstition Wilderness map.

Difficulty: Moderate.

Length: About fifteen miles.

Elevation: 3,200 to 5,600 feet.

Special attractions: Permanent stream, historic ranches, pine forest, highest point in Superstition Mountains.

Water availability: See description.

Best season: October-November, March-May.

For more information: Mesa Ranger District, P.O. Box 5800, Mesa, AZ 85201; (602) 379-6446.

Permit: None.

The hike: From Arizona 88, turn south onto Forest Road 449, approximately seven miles east of Roosevelt Dam. Drive south on the main road about seven miles to the signed trailhead, parking at the old Upper Horrel Place, a ranch which is now the Reavis Mountain School, a wilderness school. The trailhead

In the Superstition Wilderness Area, Weaver's Needle is the site of the legendary Lost Dutchman Mine, where gold is hidden within the shadow of the needle. Despite the fact that the volcanic rock in the area has a very low potential for valuable minerals, "weekend prospectors" continue the search. Bruce Grubbs

Fish Creek Canyon in the heart of the Superstitions is easily reached by taking the Apache Trail Road. Since the canyon is trailless, you probably won't encounter very many people as you hike upstream. Bruce Grubbs

One Mile

NORTH

area is privately owned; please stay on the trail. This approach road crosses Campaign Creek a number of times, and a high-clearance vehicle is advisable. The road may be impassable after a major storm.

By linking several trails, hikers can create a fine loop trip in the less-traveled, high, eastern end of the Superstition Mountains. Start by taking the signed Campaign Creek Trail (Forest Trail 256) from the trailhead less than .5 mile to the signed junction with the Reavis Gap Trail (Forest Trail 117). Take this trail west as it ascends a drainage system to Reavis Gap, a saddle at the south end of Two Bar Mountain. The area is open pinyon-juniper woodland with good views to the east. Walnut Spring, to the south on the Two Bar Ridge trail, is only a muddy seep. The Reavis Gap Trail ascends slightly over another ridge, then drops to cross Pine Creek in a stand of ponderosa pines. There is water here in the cool season and several fine campsites. Pine Creek is interesting to explore either up or downstream.

Continuing west-southwest, the Reavis Gap Trail ascends another gradual slope to a pass, then descends to meet the signed Reavis Trail (Forest Trail 109) north of Reavis Ranch. Turn south on the Reavis Trail and follow Reavis Creek upstream about a mile to the old Reavis Ranch site. Along the way, you will pass an old apple orchard which is so famous among hikers and horsepackers for its sweet fruit that it is picked clean every season.

Most people approach Reavis Ranch via the Reavis Trail, which used to be an access road to the ranch before it was sold to the Forest Service and became part of the wilderness area. There is excellent camping above and below the ranch area with water in the creek during the cool season.

From Reavis Ranch, continue south on the Reavis Trail less than a mile to the signed junction with the Fireline Trail (Forest Trail 118), where you turn left (east) and ascend into a drainage. This trail is a former firebreak built to help contain a large fire which devastated the Mound Mountain-Iron Mountain area, probably in the 1950s. Despite the fire, the area still contains large stands of ponderosa pines, a surprise to people familiar only with the lower, western Superstitions.

The trail climbs past Whiskey Spring, which is probably reliable, then climbs steeply over the ridge and down into Pine Creek . From the ridge area, it is possible to hike cross-country to the summit of Mound Mountain, the highest point in the Superstition Mountains, without encountering too much brush. Indian ruins are common in this section of the Superstitions, and you will probably find one or more if you venture off-trail. Remember to leave them undisturbed for future hikers to enjoy.

There is good camping and seasonal water at Pine Creek. The Fireline Trail continues down the creek for a short distance, then climbs over the ridge northeast of Mound Mountain and drops steeply into Campaign Creek to join the signed Campaign Creek Trail (Forest Trail 256). There is more camping here, and water during the cool season. For an enjoyable side hike, follow the Campaign Creek Trail south (right) to the saddle southwest of Pinto Peak, where fine vantage points survey the rugged Pinto Creek area.

Back at the junction with the Fireline Trail, continue north (left) on the Campaign Creek Trail as the creek gradually loses elevation and vegetation changes correspondingly. In the upper canyon, ponderosa pines are common; lower down, they are replaced by juniper and pinyon pine. Sycamores are abundant along the entire pleasant walk to the trailhead at Upper Horrel, and there are numerous places to camp.—*Bruce Grubbs*

HIKE 92 *BULL PASTURE-MOUNT AJO*

General description: A round-trip day hike in the Organ Pipe Cactus National Monument Wilderness Area.
General location: Organ Pipe Cactus National Monument.
Maps: Mt. Ajo 7.5-minute USGS quad.
Difficulty: Moderate to difficult.
Length: About 3.5 miles one way.
Elevation: 2,300 to 4,800 feet.
Special attractions: Unique desert area, rugged mountains, historic ranching area.
Water availability: None.
Best season: October through April.
For more information: Organ Pipe Cactus National Monument, Rt. 1, Box 100, Ajo, AZ 85321; (520) 387-6849.
Permit: None for dayhikes.

The hike: From the Organ Pipe Cactus National Monument headquarters (a stop at the visitor center to learn about this unique desert area is worthwhile), take the Ajo Mountain loop drive to the signed Bull Pasture trailhead, about eight miles.

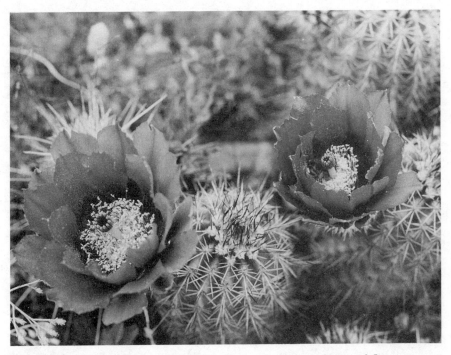

Hedgehog cactus is one of the earliest blooming cacti; the lavender-to-red flowers appear as early as March. The dark red, juicy fruits of the hedgehog cactus are eaten by birds and rodents, and the Pima Indians consider them a delicacy. Stewart Aitchison

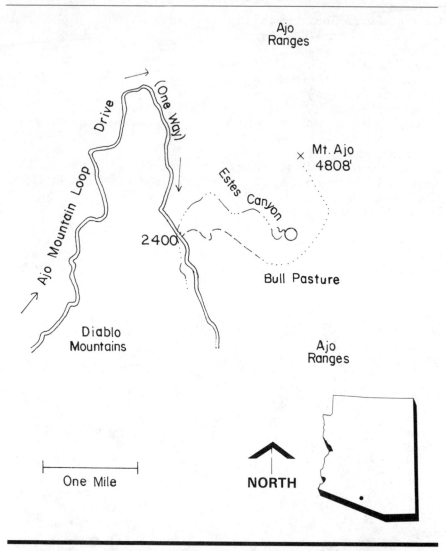

The maintained trail leaves the picnic area and climbs about a mile to a ridge overlooking Bull Pasture, a scenic basin high on the flanks of the Ajo Range. Bull Pasture was a favorite cow pasture back in the days when grazing was still allowed in the area. From the trail's end at the overlook, a rough but rewarding cross-country hike leads to the summit of Mount Ajo, at 4,808 feet the highest in the monument. Leave the end of the trail and work your way around the head of the Bull Pasture basin, moving generally east toward the steep slopes on the far side. Then head generally up and right to gain the main north-south ridgecrest. You will have to pick your way around some cliff bands. Once you have reached the ridge, it is a straightforward walk north about a mile to the summit, your turnaround point.

From the ridge and the summit, you can see far south into Mexico, west across Organ Pipe Cactus National Monument, and north and east across the Papago Indian Reservation toward rugged Baboquivari Mountain. This rugged Basin-and-Range topography is typical of southwest Arizona.—*Bruce Grubbs*

HIKE 93 *ROMERO CANYON*

General description: A moderate round-trip day hike (which may be extended) in the Pusch Ridge Wilderness Area.
General location: Coronado National Forest, northwest of Tucson.
Maps: Mt. Lemmon 7.5-minute, Oro Valley 7.5-minute USGS quads; Santa Catalina Mountains (Southern Arizona Hiking Club) map.
Difficulty: Moderate.
Length: 7.2 miles one-way to Mt. Lemmon Trail.
Elevation: 2,800 to 6,000 feet.
Special attractions: Beautiful vistas, solitude, waterfalls, and slickrock areas; vegetation from Sonoran desert to coniferous forests, all within a short distance of Tucson.

An unusual cristate form of saguaro cactus, this fan-shaped condition is an abnormal growth resulting from an injury at the apex caused by fungi, bacteria, birds, or insects. Round holes are sometimes seen near the tops of branches. These have usually been made by Gila woodpeckers or flickers for nests. Afterwards these cavitities may be occupied by elf owls. Stewart Aitchison

HIKE 93 *ROMERO CANYON*

Catalina
State
Park

Day Use
Area
2800'
P.

Romero Canyon

Mt. Lemmon Trail

Romero Pass

Wash

La Ceñada

89N

Montrose Canyon

Pusch Peak

Pusch Ridge

Pima Canyon

To Metro Tucson
Oracle Road

Ina Rd.

One Mile

NORTH

Water availability: Unreliable and quality questionable; pack your own.
Best season: October to May; summer is unbearably hot.
For more information: Santa Catalina Ranger District, 5700 N. Sabino
Canyon Rd., Tucson, AZ 85715; (520) 749-8700.
Permit: None—however, there is an entry fee at the entrance station to
Catalina State Park.

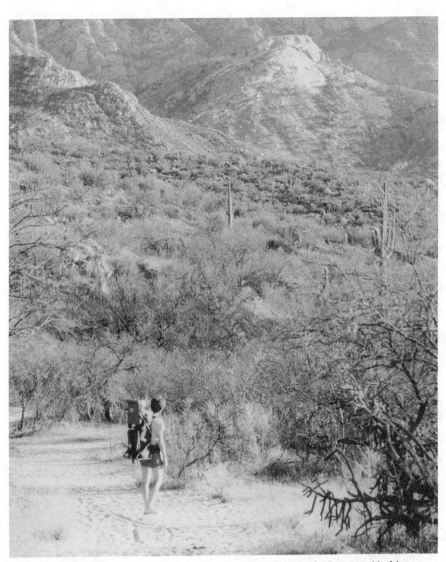

The Romero Canyon trailhead is located in Catalina State Park. Stewart Aitchison

The hike: To find the trailhead, go north on Oracle Road approximately six miles from the Ina intersection. Turn right into Catalina State Park (where a nominal entry fee is required) and continue to the Day Use Area. Park here and walk across the streambed just southeast of the information center. Trails are marked and a map of the park area is available at the entrance station.

This trail will give you access to the major north-south region of the Santa Catalina Mountains, just north of Tucson. It also provides access to many other trails within the area (such as Mt. Lemmon, Wilderness of Rocks, Cathedral Rock, Canada Del Oro, and Sutherland, among others). The trail is marked at the trailhead and continues to be well-marked, at least as far as the junction with the Mt. Lemmon Trail. It maintains a fairly steep grade but is not tortuous, and hikers can always shorten the trip by turning around before reaching the turnaround point at the Mt. Lemmon Trail intersection.

The hiking in this area is rewarding and dramatic. Many flowers bloom in the spring and you can expect to find water in the main canyons. By summer, though, the water is gone. This trail offers a great respite from the hustle and bustle of the city and excellent access to the more remote areas of the Pusch Ridge Wilderness, which was set aside in 1978 primarily for the protection of critical lambing grounds for bighorn sheep.—*Bill Williams* □

Although only minutes from Tucson, the Pima Canyon trail soon takes hikers into a wilderness setting. Stewart Aitchison

HIKE 94 *PIMA CANYON*

General description: A round-trip day hike into the Pusch Ridge Wilderness Area.

General location: Just north of Tucson city limits, near the Ina Road-Oracle Road intersection.

Maps: Tucson North 7.5-minute USGS quad; Santa Catalina Mountains (Southern Arizona Hiking Club) map.

Difficulty: Moderate.

Length: 7.6 miles to junction with Kimball Trail.

Elevation: 2,900 to 7,200 feet.

Special attractions: Wilderness solitude within a short distance of the Tucson metro area; flowing stream from winter through spring; beautiful desert riparian habitat.

Water availability: Unreliable and of questionable quality.

Best season: October to May; summer too hot.

For more information: Santa Catalina Ranger District, 5700 N. Sabino Canyon Road, Tucson, AZ 85715; (520) 749-8700.

Permit: None.

The hike: Although the trailhead is only a few minutes drive from downtown Tucson, within fifteen minutes of hiking you are isolated from the city. The trail is well-marked and popular, providing wonderful views of the Sonoran Desert.

To locate the trailhead, drive north on Oracle Road a mile from the Ina-Oracle intersection and then turn right onto Magee Road. Drive to the end of Magee Road (about 1.5 miles) and follow the signed, major trail (Forest Trail 62) eastward toward the mouth of Pima Canyon. The trail enters the canyon on the left side of the streambed, then meanders up the canyon, crossing the streambed many times. Nevertheless, it is easy to follow all the way to the signed Kimball Trail junction, your turnaround point. The length of your trip up Pima Canyon is only limited by your desire and time. During the winter months, there is a wide variety of birdlife in the area. Also, keep a lookout for deer and bighorn sheep.

When there is water in the intermittent stream, this is a great place to enjoy the warm weather. This day hike ends at the junction with Forest Trail 42. From that junction, however, a number of other trails lead into the wilderness area, any of which allow for longer backpack trips into the higher, coniferous forests and provide great views.—*Bill Williams*

89N

Kimball Trail

Pusch Ridge

Pima Canyon Spring

Mt. Kimball

Window Rock
The Window

Oracle Rd.

Pusch Peak

Pima Canyon

Magee Rd.

℗ 2900'

Ina Rd.

To Metro Tucson

◯ Parking Area

One Mile

NORTH

HIKE 95 *MICA MOUNTAIN*

General description: An overnight, round-trip backpack on the main trail to the highest point of the Rincon Mountains in the Saguaro National Monument Wilderness Area.

General location: Trailhead is at the east end of Speedway Boulevard in Tucson.

Maps: Tanque Verde Peak 7.5-minute, Mica Mountain 7.5-minute USGS quad; Rincon Mountains (Southern Arizona Hiking Club) map.

Difficulty: Moderate; good, well-marked trail.

Length: From the end of Speedway to the tower on Mica Mountain is 12.4 miles one way.

Elevation: 2,748 to 8,666 feet.

Special attractions: The only high mountain range left in Arizona which is not topped by a road; wonderful wilderness.

The desert bighorn sheep is more dependent on water then many desert mammals. Therefore one of the best places to observe them is at a spring or a natural rock tank called tinajas in southern Arizona. They try to drink at least once a day, usually in the early morning. Stewart Aitchison

HIKE 95 *MICA MOUNTAIN*

East End of
Speedway
2748'

Douglas Springs
△ Campgroud
× 4680

Italian Spring

Mica MT
8664'

Helens Dome
8364' ×

Manning
Camp △ 7950'
×

Cowhead Saddle
6100'

One Mile

NORTH

Water availability: Permanent water only at Italian Springs and Manning Camp. Douglas Springs (five miles from the trailhead) have seasonal water except in late spring and late fall.

Best season: Spring, fall, winter; summer temperatures can be brutal.

For more information: Saguaro National Monument, Old Spanish Trail, Route 8, Box 695, Tucson, AZ 85730; (520) 296-8576.

Permit: Required for overnight use. Camping only in designated campgrounds: Douglas Springs and Manning Camp. No pets or firearms allowed.

The hike: Since no hunting is allowed in the Monument, it abounds with wildlife. It is not uncommon for quiet hikers to see deer, javelina, or coyotes.

For purposes of this hike description, the Mica Mountain Trail can be divided into three segments, each with an elevation gain of about 2,000 feet. From the end of Speedway to Douglas Springs, the vegetation typifies the Sonoran Desert. The trail climbs 2,000 feet in about three miles and then remains fairly level for the next two miles. Hikers may want to take a nice side trip to a waterfall about 1.5 miles from the trailhead as you enter a mesquite thicket, the falls can be seen on the right. Where the map shows "Aquila Corral," a well-used horse trail leads to the fall's base.

From Douglas Spring, the trail climbs to Cowhead Saddle. About a mile from the campground, you enter a lovely forested canyon. If you are low on water, this is the last place to fill up before reaching the top—a small, stagnant pool, but still better than being without.

As you climb out of the canyon, the Cowhead (which looks more like a sitting camel) is directly in front of you. From a trail intersection at the saddle, take the trail to Mica, which climbs on the ridge to the east.

Just when the ridge seems like it will never end, the trail turns and drops into a beautiful drainage forested with ponderosa pines. The trail continues up the drainage, past a huge rock outcropping on the left—Helen's Dome—and to a fork.

At the fork you can relax. You are now only a couple hundred feet lower than the top, your turnaround point. You also have a choice of which way to go to Mica.

The North Slope Trail goes through lush vegetation for two miles until it comes to Italian Springs, a permanent source of water. From the spring, it climbs south to join another trail. Going east on this trail will take you to Mica Secondary. The view from here is worth the few minutes it takes to climb it.

Heading back west, the trail goes to Mica Tower. The view from the tower is superb. Unfortunately, since the tower is no longer in use, the Park Service has enclosed the base with barbed wire and has removed the lower stairs.

There is also an easier route to Mica from the fork near Helen's Dome. Take the trail to the south, which leads to Manning Camp. After .2 mile, there is an another fork. From here to the tower is only 1.4 miles. This trail goes by Spud Rock, which is only a few feet lower than Mica. Again the view is worth the short, easy scramble.

There is no register at the summit, but there is one at Manning Camp. A nice loop hike also follows the trail east from the tower for about .1 mile. The trail coming from the southwest takes you right to Manning.

The cabin at Manning Camp was built by Arizona pioneer Levi Manning as a summer home in 1905. Reportedly, Mrs. Manning had a piano in it. Today, it is used only by Park Service personnel. There is water throughout the year in the little lake near the cabin.—*Sid Hirsh*

HIKE 96 *SYCAMORE CANYON*

General description: A round-trip day hike into the Pajarita Wilderness Area.
General location: Fifteen miles west of Nogales.
Maps: Ruby 7.5-minute USGS quad; Coronado National Forest (Nogales Ranger District) map.
Difficulty: Moderate.
Length: About six miles one way.
Elevation: 3,500 to 4,000 feet.
Special attractions: A botanist's and birder's paradise.
Water availability: Permanent stream.
Best season: All year.
For more information: Nogales Ranger District, 2251 N. Grand Ave., Nogales, AZ 85621; (520) 281-2296.
Permit: None.

The hike: Drive about fifty-five miles south of Tucson on Interstate nineteen and then exit onto Arizona 289. Go about twenty miles and turn left at the Sycamore Canyon sign. The parking area is .5 mile down this road at Hank and Yank Spring, the site of an old post-Civil War ranch that was founded by Hank Hewitt and Yank Bartlett.

HIKE 96 *SYCAMORE CANYON*

There is no "official" trail but rather just a route going downstream. To avoid wading, especially at high water, you may have to do some fancy footwork along cliffs and ledges. Avoid this route, however, if there is any chance of flooding.

This pleasant walk along the streambed eventually ends at the Mexican border, some six miles distant, marked by an old barbed wire fence. There are a number of swimming holes to divert your attention.

The stream is home to a rare desert fish called the Sonoran chub. But don't break out your fishing pole. These fish are usually no more than four inches long and, besides, are protected by law.

Part of the canyon has been set aside as the Goodding Reasearch Natural Area. Botanists have identified more than 624 species of plants in the Sycamore Canyon area; many of them are rare and endangered. Several have "disjointed ranges," which means that they are found only in scattered, isolated populations. One of the more intriguing such species is a fern which only exists only in the Himalayas, Mexico, and here at Sycamore Canyon.

In addition to rare species, sycamores and Arizona walnuts thrive along the creek and juniper and oak dot drier slopes. A few saguaro stand on the warmer, south-facing slopes. Look for western coral-bean, a large shrub with light brown bark containing longitudinal white lines. The bright red seeds of the western coral-bean are poisonous, and in Mexico are strung together to make necklaces.

Birders will have a marvelous time along this creek, especially in spring and summer. Black phoebe, vermilion flycatcher, red-tailed hawk, common black-hawk, several kinds of herons, and woodpeckers are only a few of more than 130 species of birds that frequent the area.

Hikers also may encounter coatimundis. These Mexican relatives of the raccoon often congregate in bands of a dozen individuals or more and are most active during the day. They are omnivorous, with a tough nose pad which aids in rooting for grubs and tubers. Included in their diet are fruits, nuts, bird eggs, lizards, scorpions and tarantulas.—*Stewart Aitchison, John Nelson, Dale Shewalter*

HIKE 97 *MOUNT WRIGHTSON*

General description: A round-trip day hike into the Mount Wrightson Wilderness Area.
General location: Thirty-five miles south of Tucson.
Maps: Mount Wrightson 7.5-minute USGS quad; Coronado National Forest (Santa Rita Mountain) map.
Difficulty: Difficult.
Length: About 6.5 miles one way.
Elevation: 5,400 to 9,453 feet.
Special attractions: Fantastic birding, great vistas.
Water availability: Sprung Spring, Bellows Spring, and Baldy Spring may be dry.
Best season: Spring through early winter.
For more information: Nogales Ranger District, 2251 N. Grand Ave., Nogales, AZ 85621; (520) 281-2296.
Permit: None.

The hike: Drive south from Tucson on Interstate 19. About four miles south of Green Valley, exit the Interstate onto the Continental/Madera Canyon Road. Follow the signs to the upper end of Madera Canyon and the Roundup Picnic Area parking lot. The trail (Forest Trail 134) begins at the north end of the parking area.

To (19)

△ Bog Springs Campground

End of
Madera Canyon Road

℗ 5440'

One Mile

NORTH

Sprung Spring

☿ Bellows Spring

Baldy Spring

☿

9453'
Mt. ✕
Wrightson

☿

⚲

Josephine Saddle

This hike begins by following a tributary of Madera Canyon. Here in the riparian habitat of walnut, sycamore, and velvet ash, you may see solitary vireo, acorn woodpeckers, Mexican jays, black-headed grosbeaks, red-shafted flickers, western tanagers, sulphur-bellied flycatchers, yellow-eyed juncos, and the rare elegant trogon. More than 170 species of birds have been recorded in this area. The trail crosses the creek and ascends through silverleaf oaks, Arizona white oaks, Emory oaks, Arizona madrone, and alligator junipers.

Just before reaching Josephine Saddle, where three Boy Scouts died of hypothermia in November of 1958, you encounter unreliable Sprung Spring. Turn left at the saddle onto Forest Trail 78, go about a .25 mile and turn left again onto Forest Trail 94. The right fork (Forest Trail 78) is a longer but less steep route to the summit.

You soon come to Bellows Spring, which may be dry. The trail proceeds up to Baldy Saddle. From the saddle head south. The route climbs through Mexican white pine and Douglas fir and finally switchbacks to the open summit. You are treated to terrific views of the Santa Ritas and surrounding desert. The Mount Hopkins telescope is visible to the west.

You can return by taking the trail (Forest Trail 78) that goes around the east and south side of the mountain and intersects your ascent route just before reaching Josephine Saddle. Baldy Spring, located along this section, is about as reliable as the other springs. Check with the Forest Service before relying on these water sources.—*Stewart Aitchison*

HIKE 98 *SUGARLOAF MOUNTAIN*

General description: A round-trip day hike to one of the highest viewpoints in the Chiricahua National Monument Wilderness Area.
General location: One hundred miles east of Tucson.
Maps: Cochise Head 7.5-minute USGS quad; National Monument brochure.
Difficulty: Easy.
Length: One mile one way.
Elevation: 6,800 to 7,305 feet.
Special attractions: Spectacular view of the Chiricahua National Monument Wilderness Area.
Water availability: None.
Best season: All year.
For more information: Chiricahua National Monument, Dos Cabezas Star Route, Box 6500, Willcox, AZ 85643; (520) 824-3560.
Permit: None.

The hike: Turn south off of Interstate 10 at the Willcox exit some 80 miles east of Tucson. From here, Arizona 186 winds through the old section of Willcox and then travels southeast for thirty miles to the monument entrance.

An alternate route on the east side of the Chiricahuas goes through the town of Portal. Turn off of U.S. 80 and follow Forest Road 42 over the mountains to the monument entrance. This road is occasionally blocked by snow during the winter.

The Chiricahuas are on a par with Bryce and Zion canyons for the beauty and spectacular nature of their geology. Your drive from the monument entrance to the trailhead takes you through lush Bonita Canyon and ascends toward Massai Point. Approximately 5.5 miles from the monument headquarters is a turn-off to the Sugarloaf Mountain parking area.

Your trail is visible from the upper parking lot, and leads a mile to the top of Sugarloaf, your turnaround point, which offers an incredible view of the monument and the surrounding area. On all sides are the sculpted and frac-tured volcanic rhyolite formations that the Chiricahuas are famous for.

The monument boasts seven different varieties of oak, as well as pines, cypress, fir, and juniper. The Chiricahuas are the northern limit for many plants and animals otherwise endemic to Mexico. Mixed with woodlands are yuccas, agave, and sotols. Javelina are quite common, as are whitetail deer. Many birds breed in or migrate through the monument, including a number of humm-ingbirds and exotic species such as the rose-throated becard and elegant trogon.

This area was one of the strongholds for Geronimo's band of Chiricahua Apaches. Fort Bowie is a short drive from the monument, and the National Park Service has a small interpretive station at the remains of the old fort.— *Steve Gustafson* □

HIKE 99 *RHYOLITE CANYON-SARA DEMING CANYON*

General description: A round-trip day hike into the Chiricahua National Monument Wilderness Area.
General location: One hundred miles east of Tucson.
Maps: Cochise Head 7.5-minute USGS quad; National Monument brochure.
Difficulty: Moderate.
Length: About three miles one way to the Heart of the Rocks area.
Elevation: 5,400 to 6,800 feet.
Special attractions: Strange rock formations and abundant wildlife.
Water availability: None.
Best season: All year.
For more information: Chiricahua National Monument, Dos Cabezas Star Route, Box 6500, Willcox, AZ 85643; (520) 824-3560.
Permit: None.

The hike: This trail begins at the Chiricahua National Monument visitor center parking lot. It climbs out of lower Bonita Canyon into the upper reaches of Rhyolite Canyon. At the 1.5-mile point, take the right fork, the Sara Deming Canyon Trail. Another 1.5 miles brings you to the Heart of the Rocks area, a land of strange balanced rocks and fanciful shapes. A signed one-mile-long trail loops through the Heart of the Rocks, which you may want to take before heading back.

These unusual rock formations are carved out of rhyolite, a type of rock formed when white-hot volcanic material piles up in layers and welds itself together. Later mountain uplifting caused the rhyolite to fracture into definite patterns. Along the vertical cracks and planes of horizontal weakness, erosion by weathering and running water began to shape the rock into the formations we see today.—*Chiricahua National Monument*

HIKE 100 *CHIRICAHUA PEAK*

General description: An overnight round-trip backpack to the summit of the Chiricahua Wilderness Area (which is different from the Chiricahua National Monument Wilderness Area named in the previous two hike descriptions).
General location: One hundred miles east of Tucson.
Maps: Chiricahua Peak 7.5-minute, Rustler Park 7.5-minute USGS quads; Coronado National Forest (Chiricahua Mountains) map.
Difficulty: Difficult.
Length: About seven miles one way.
Elevation: 6,300 to 9,796 feet.
Special attractions: Possible sightings of mountain lions; Mexican wolves; Rocky Mountain, Sonoran, and Chihuahuan species of birds.
Water availability: Anita Spring is usually running.
Best season: Spring through fall.

For more information: Douglas Ranger District, Rt. 1, Box 228R, Leslie Canyon Road, Douglas, AZ 85607; (520) 364-3468.

Permit: None.

The hike: To reach this wonderful hike, drive about seventy miles east of Tucson on Interstate 10. Exit at U.S. 666 and head south twenty-five miles to Arizona 181. Drive east on 181 about twelve miles and turn onto Forest Road 41. Nine miles will bring you to a signed, short spur road to the Saulsbury Canyon Trail (Forest Trail 263).

The trail begins by ambling up through a lovely forest of oak, Apache and Chihuahua pine, and Arizona cypress. The route steepens, but you are treated to magnificent views across the wilderness and Sulphur Springs Valley. As you continue to climb, the vegetation will change to Douglas fir and Engelmann spruce and finally some quaking aspen.

Turn right at the signed Crest Trail (Forest Trail 270) and walk south toward Round Park. Water is usually available at Booger Springs, although it may be dry in a drought year. Farther south you come to Anita Park and Anita Spring, which like Booger Spring may be dry. Otherwise this is a good campsite.

From Anita Park, it is another mile to the summit of Chiricahua Peak, your turnaround point. Unfortunately, the dense forest blocks most of the view.

This area does not have the strange rock formations found in the nearby Chiricahua National Monument, but the amazing variety of plants and wildlife should satisfy any naturalist. Mexican wolves are known to occasionally enter the area and there are persistent rumors of Mexican grizzlies. There are definitely black bear and mountain lion in this range.

Many birds utilize this area, not only typical Arizona and Mexican species but also some Eastern species such as warblers passing through on their migrations to and from Mexico.—*Stewart Aitchison*

The remarkable rhyolite pillars in the Chiricahua National Monument Wilderness Area are the result of fused volcanic magma being eroded into columns. At least eight eruptions are responsible for the accumulation of nearly two thousand feet of volcanic debris. Stewart Aitchison

HIKE 100 *CHIRICAHUA PEAK*

Turkey Creek
Ranger Station
FR 41

To ←
State Highway 181
Turkey Creek
Campground

6150'

△ Morse
Canyon
Campground

9666'
Fly Pk.
Lookout

Cima Park

Anita
Spring

Chiricahua
Peak
9796'

9357'
Mount Vista Lookout

NORTH

One Mile

HIKE 101   *WABAYUMA PEAK*

General description: A round-trip day hike to the top of 7,601-foot Wabayuma Peak within the Wabayuma Peak Wilderness Area.

General location: Thirty miles southeast of Kingman in the Hualapai Mountains.

Maps: Wabayuma Peak 7.5-minute USGS quad.

Difficulty: Moderate with some cross-country travel.

Length: About three miles one way.

Elevation: 6,047 to 7,601 feet.

Special attractions: Spectacular views of the nearby mountain ranges and the Mohave Desert.

Water availability: None.

Best season: Late spring through fall.

For more information: Kingman Resource Area, Bureau of Land Management, 2475 Beverly Avenue, Kingman, AZ 86401; (520) 757-3161.

Permit: None.

The hike: Wabayuma Peak is the second-tallest peak in the Hualapai Mountain Range. The mountains were named after the Hualapai Indians, the people of the tall pines, a Yuman Indian group who used to live in the nearby valleys and along a portion of the lower Colorado River. The steep but fairly easy hike to the top of this peak rewards hikers with expansive views of the surrounding country. There is no water source on this trail, so bring enough.

The biggest struggle on this hike is getting to the trailhead. A four-wheel-drive vehicle is recommended. Snow may block the northern approach road until late spring.

To reach the trailhead, follow the Hualapai Mountain Road out of Kingman. Drive through Hualapai Mountain County Park and past the recently built houses. Leave the pavement after 12.6 miles, turning right onto the dirt road. The small wooden signs for Flag Mine Road and Wild Cow Springs mark your turn. In another 3.7 miles, you reach Wild Cow Spring campground. The road continues through the campground and then climbs steeply up the hill. Stay on the main road that follows the ridgeline to the south for another 13.5 miles. Park at the shallow pullout opposite the jeep trail that takes off steeply up the hill to the northwest . The trailhead is 29.8 miles from the start of the Hualapai Mountain Road.

A shorter but much rougher approach leaves Interstate 40 at the Alamo Road in Yucca. After 1.4 miles, turn left on the Borianna Mine Road. Follow this rocky road up the Copper Creek drainage, past the relic Borianna Mine (at mile 17.3), up the steep grade, and along the ridge for another three miles.

The first two miles of your hiking trail follow an old jeep road that is blocked by a fallen tree. Manzanita, shrub live oak, and banana yucca line the trail. This warmer, southern exposure is a major influence on the types of plants that grow here. After the initial climb, the trail crosses some cooler, shaded pockets. An immediate transition to ponderosa pine trees occurs. As the trail heads west, good views of Hualapai Peak to the north appear. The rocky outcrop of Wabayuma Peak is visible to the west.

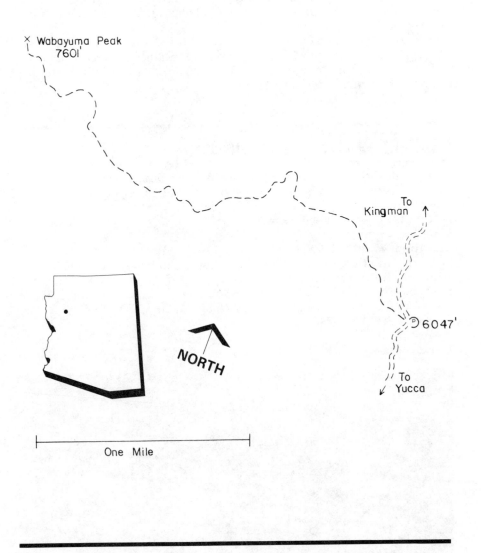

Wabayuma Peak
7601'

To
Kingman

6047'

To
Yucca

NORTH

One Mile

After approximately two miles, the jeep track drops down into a small clearing and then makes a sharp bend to the north. A short stretch of fence line on your left as the trail descends is your other guidemark. At this bend look for a narrow trail heading northwest up the shrub-filled slope. Two small cairns mark the start of this final ascent.

The trail switchbacks quickly up the slope; pink and yellow rocks serve as steps along the way. Deer use is evident on the trail. When the trail enters a grove of ponderosa pine, notched blaze marks keep you on track.

As the trail crosses the saddle and starts to descend, it is time to head cross-country. The exposed rocky point to the south is only four feet lower than the summit, but it is a much easier scramble. The second peak visible to the north is the actual summit of Wabayuma Peak. After bushwhacking, a steep rock climb will put you on top. Hedgehog cactus are growing in the cracks of the rocks, so careful placement of hands and feet is essential for a safe ascent.

From the top, spectacular views of the Black Mountains to the west, Hualapai Peak to the north, the Aquarius Montains to the east, and the rest of the Hualapai Mountains to the south reward your climb. Return the way you came.—*Rudi Lambrechtse*

HIKE 102 *PALM CANYON*

General description: A round-trip day hike to a desert oasis.
General location: Twenty-two miles southeast of Quartzite.
Maps: Palm Canyon 7.5-minute USGS quad.
Difficulty: Easy (cross-country).
Length: .75 miles one way.
Elevation: 2,100 to 2,500 feet.
Special attractions: Native palm trees growing in a desert canyon oasis.
Water availability: None.
Best season: All year, but very hot in summer.
For more information: Kofa National Wildlife Refuge, P.O. Box 6290, Yuma, AZ 85364; (520) 783-7861.
Permit: None.
Wilderness status: FWS Wilderness Study Area.

The rugged Kofa Mountains offer refuge for the desert bighorn sheep. Bruce Grubbs

HIKE 102 PALM CANYON

To Quartzite

KOFA GAME RANGE

95

Palm Canyon

2100'   2500'

First Grove of Palms

Interpretive Sign About Palm Canyon

To Yuma

One Mile

NORTH

The hike: To reach Palm Canyon drive either nineteen miles south of Quartzite or 62 miles north of Yuma on Arizona 95. Turn off onto a signed dirt road that heads east toward the Kofa Range. At the Kofa National Wildlife Refuge boundary you may pick up a brochure describing the area.

A .75-mile walk up the wash at the end of the road will bring you to the palms. These are California Washingtonia palms. In Arizona, they only occur in Palm Canyon and in other deep, narrow canyons of the Kofa Mountains. Also keep watch for bighorn sheep.

Today the species is commonly planted as an ornamental in southern Arizona, but this native population was not discovered until 1923. In southeastern California, where this species is more common, the fruits were gathered and eaten by Indians. The botanist who named this palm dedicated it to President George Washington.

In the 1890s, Charles Eichelberger discovered the King of Arizona Mine in this rugged range. To mark company property, he had a branding iron that read "K of A." Later when a post office name was being discussed, someone remembered the brand and the name Kofa resulted.—*Stewart Aitchison* □

AFTERWORD

Arizona's wilderness challenge

Arizona is a land of many wild places. Its snow-covered peaks, lush canyons, and pristine deserts call out to us. There is, perhaps, no other place in the lower 48 states where one can better experience the grandeur and raw beauty of wilderness. It is for this reason that so many of us choose to visit or live in Arizona.

The lure of wilderness is an important part of the western mystique. The American West was a symbol of hope for the brave and adventurous. It was a place that rewarded the strong and self-reliant. It was a place where you could 'get away' from the negative qualities of civilized life. And most important, it was a place where you could be free. The Wild West is gone, but the dream it represents lingers in our western wildernesses.

We are not the only ones who need or use those wild places. There are thousands of plant and animal species which make up the natural environment, plants and animals which evolved through the ages into an intricate web of life. It is their world we visit when we enter the wilderness; it is their natural order that many of us find so appealing and perplexing.

However, these wild lands are disappearing. Arizona is now one of the fastest-growing states in the country. As our numbers increase, so do our demands for more housing, farms, mines, roads, and similar developments. Something has to give. That something is too often the natural environment.

The solution is to set aside a few wild places now. This is not a new idea. President Theodore Roosevelt started a tradition of conservation with the creation of Grand Canyon National Park, the first of many national parks in Arizona. The Forest Service pondered the idea of wilderness for another forty years. In 1964, Congress adopted the Wilderness Act and officially designated certain lands as parts of a national wilderness system. In 1976, Congress passed the Organic Act, a similar mechanism, so that Bureau of Land Management lands can also be designated wilderness.

So where are we now? With the passage of the 1984 Arizona Wilderness Bill, about one million acres of primarily Forest Service lands were designated as official wilderness. This brought the total to about two million acres or less than three percent of our state.

However as the 101st Congress neared adjournment in October, 1990, it passed the Arizona Desert Wilderness Act. This important, precedent-setting piece of legislation is the first major wilderness act designed for any western state that has addressed the issue of Bureau of Land Management land on a statewide basis.

The act designated slightly over one million acres of BLM wilderness and 1.3 million acres of wilderness in Havasu, Imperial, Kofa, and Cabeza Prieta National Wildlife Refuges. It also added 12,710 acres to the existing Aravaipa Canyon Wilderness and established the 20,900-acre Gila Box Riparian National Conservation Area.

Arizona now has over four million acres of designated wilderness.

Hikers and backpackers have always been important to the wilderness movement. Their love of wild places fuels conservation efforts. They know the areas which should be protected and why. They spend long hours learning about their favorite areas: mapping boundaries, resolving conflicts of interest, and working with federal agency personnel. Some of them educate and entertain the public with beautiful slide shows and exciting stories of their adventures. And when it comes down to the nitty gritty, they lobby for "their" wilderness by writing letters to and meeting with their elected officials. If an area is fortunate enough to obtain wilderness designation, then hikers make sure that it is managed in accordance with the wilderness ethic.

I invite you to visit a piece of wild Arizona. You will discover many things about yourself as well as the natural world. And I hope you will help us preserve and protect this valuable resource.—*Dawson Henderson*

(Dawson Henderson is the former coordinator for the Arizona Wilderness Coalition, a non-profit organization working on wilderness and public lands issues. For more information, write The Wilderness Society, Southwest Regional Office, 234 N. Central Avenue, Phoenix, AZ 85004.)

RESOURCES

LOCAL HIKING CLUBS AND CONSERVATION ORGANIZATIONS

Arizona Mountaineering Club, P.O. Box 1695, Phoenix, AZ 85001

Arizona Nature Conservancy, 300 E. University Blvd., Suite 230, Tucson, AZ 85705 (520) 622-3861

Central Arizona Hiking Club, 1026 N. 9th St., Phoenix, AZ 85006

Grand Canyon Trust, Rt. 4, Box 718, Flagstaff, Az 86001 (520) 774-7488

Green Valley Hiking Club, P.O. Box 1074, Green Valley, AZ 85622

Huachuca Hiking Club, 1515 Hummingbird Lane, Sierra Vista, AZ 85635

Maricopa Audubon Society, 4619 East Arcadia Lane, Phoenix, AZ 85018 (602) 959-0052

National Parks & Conservation Association, P.O. Box 67, Cottonwood, AZ 86326 (602) 634-5758

Northern Arizona Audubon Society, P.O. Box 1496, Sedona, AZ 86339 (520) 779-3855

Sierra Club, Grand Canyon Chapter, 5121 N. 13th Avenue, Phoenix, AZ 85013 (602) 279-9427

Tucson Audubon Society, 30-A North Tucson Blvd., Tucson, AZ 85716 (602) 629-0510

FEDERAL AND STATE AGENCIES
Bureau of Land Management,

Arizona State Office, 3707 N. 7th St., Phoenix, AZ 85014 (602) 650-0200

Arizona Strip District Office, 345 E. Riverside Dr., St. George, UT 84770 (801) 628-4491

Kingman Resource Area, 2475 Beverly Ave., Kingman, AZ 86401 (520) 757-3161

Phoenix District Office, 2015 West Deer Valley Road, Phoenix, AZ 85027 (602) 780-8090

Safford District Office, 425 E. 4th Street, Safford, AZ 85546 (520) 428-4040

Yuma District Office, P.O. Box 5680, 3150 S. Winsor Ave., Yuma, AZ 85364 (520) 726-6300

National Park Service

Canyon de Chelly National Monument, P.O. Box 588, Chinle, AZ 86503 (520) 674-5510

Chiricahua National Monument, Dos Cabezas Star Route, Box 6500, Willcox, AZ 85643 (520) 824-3560

Grand Canyon National Park, P.O. Box 129, Grand Canyon, AZ 86023 (520) 638-7888

Navajo National Monument, HC 71 Box 3, Tonalea, AZ 86044 (520) 672-2366/2367

Organ Pipe Cactus National Monument, Rt. 1 Box 100, Ajo, AZ 85321 (520) 387-6849

Rainbow Bridge National Monument, P.O. Box 1507, Page, AZ 86040 (520) 645-2471

Saguaro National Park, Old Spanish Trail Route 8, Box 695, Tucson, AZ 85730 (520) 670-6680; (520) 883-6366

National wildlife refuges

Kofa National Wildlife Refuge, P.O. Box 6290, Yuma, AZ 85364 (520) 783-7861

Tribal governments

White Mountain Apache Enterprise Fort Apache Indian Reservation, P.O. Box 218, Whiteriver, AZ 85941 (520) 338-4385

Havasupai Indian Reservation, Havasupai Tourist Enterprise, Supai, AZ 86435 (520) 448-2121

Navajo Indian Reservation, Recreation Resource Department, P.O. Box 9000, Window Rock, AZ 86515 (520) 871-6447

United States Forest Service

Apache-Sitgreaves National Forest, P.O. Box 640, Springerville, AZ 85938 (520) 333-4301

Alpine Ranger District, P.O. Box 469, Alpine, AZ 85920 (520) 339-4384

Clifton Ranger District, Box 698, Clifton, AZ 85533 (520) 687-1303

Chevelon Ranger District, HC-61 Box 1, Winslow, AZ 86047 (520) 289-2471

Heber Ranger District, P.O. Box 968, Overgaard, AZ 85933 (520) 535-4481

Lakeside Ranger District, P.O. Box 488, Lakeside, AZ 85929 (520) 368-5111

Springerville Ranger District, P.O. Box 760, Springerville, AZ 86938 (520) 333-4301

Coconino National Forest, 2323 E. Greenlaw Lane, Flagstaff, AZ 86004 (520) 527-3600

Beaver Creek Ranger District, HC-64 Box 240, Rimrock, AZ 86335 (520) 567-4501

Blue Ridge Ranger District, HC-31 Box 300, Happy Jack, AZ 86024 (520) 477-2255

Long Valley Ranger District, HC-31 Box 68, Happy Jack, AZ 86024 (520) 354-2480, 354-2216

Mormon Lake Ranger District, 4825 S. Lake Mary Road, Flagstaff, AZ 86001 (520) 774-1147

Peaks Ranger District, 5075 N. Hwy. 89, Flagstaff, AZ 86004 (520) 526-0866

Sedona Ranger District, P.O. Box 300, Sedona, AZ 86336 (520) 282-4119

Coronado National Forest, Federal Building 301 West Congress, Tucson, AZ 85701 (520) 670-4552

Douglas Ranger District, Rt. 1, Box 228R Leslie Canyon Road, Douglas, AZ 85607 (520) 364-3231

Nogales Ranger District, 2251 N. Grand Ave., Nogales, AZ 85621 (520) 281-2296

Safford Ranger District, P.O. Box 709, Safford, AZ 85546 (520) 428-4150

Santa Catalina Ranger District, 5700 N. Sabino Canyon Rd., Tucson, AZ 85715 (520) 749-8700

Sierra Vista Ranger District, 5990 S. Hwy 92, Sierra Vista, AZ 85635 (520) 378-0311

Kaibab National Forest, 800 S. 6th Street, Williams, AZ 86046 (520) 635-8200

Chalender Ranger District, 501 W. Bill Williams Ave., Williams, AZ 86046 (520) 635-2676

North Kaibab Ranger District, P.O. Box 248, Fredonia, AZ 86022 (520) 643-7395

Tusayan Ranger District, P.O. Box 3088, Tusayan, AZ 86023 (520) 638-2443

Williams Ranger District, Rt. 1, Box 142, Williams, AZ 86046 (520) 635-2633

Prescott National Forest, 344 South Cortez, Street P.O. Box 2549, Prescott, AZ 86303 (520) 445-1762

Bradshaw Ranger District, 2230 E. Hwy 69, Prescott, AZ 86301 (520) 445-7253

Chino Valley Ranger District, P.O. Box 485, Chino Valley, AZ 86323 (520) 636-2302

Verde Ranger District, Box 670, Camp Verde, AZ 86322 (520) 567-4121

Tonto National Forest, 2324 E. McDowell Rd., Phoenix, AZ 85006 (602) 225-5200

Cave Creek Ranger District, P.O. Box 5068, Carefree, AZ 85331 (602) 488-3441

Globe Ranger District, Rt. 1, Box 33, Globe, AZ 85501 (520) 425-7189

Mesa Ranger District, P.O. Box 5800, Mesa, AZ 85201 (602) 379-6446

Payson Ranger District, P.O. Box 100, Payson, AZ 85541 (520) 474-7900

Pleasant Valley Ranger District, P.O. Box 450, Young, AZ 85554 (520) 462-3311

Tonto Basin Ranger District, P.O. Box 649, Roosevelt, AZ 85545 (520) 467-2236

State offices

Arizona State Parks, 1300 West Washington, Phoenix, AZ 85007 (602) 542-4174.

FURTHER READING

Aitchison, Stewart. *Oak Creek Canyon and the Red Rock Country Of Arizona: A Natural History and Trail Guide.* Stillwater Canyon Press: Flagstaff, Arizona, 1978.

Aitchison, Stewart. *A Naturalist's Guide to Hiking the Grand Canyon.* Prentice-Hall: Englewood Cliffs, New Jersey, 1985.

Aitchison, Stewart. *A Guide to Exploring Oak Creek and the Sedona Area.* RNM Press, Salt Lake City, Utah 1989.

Annerino, John. *Hiking the Grand Canyon.* Sierra Club Books: San Francisco. 1986.

Bowman, Eldon. *A Guide to the General Crook Trail.* Museum of Northern Arizona Press: Flagstaff, Arizona, 1978.

Bunker, Gerald. *Arizona's Northland Trails.* La Siesta Press: Glendale, California, 1972.

Butchart, Harvey. *Grand Canyon Treks.* La Siesta Press: Glendale, California, 1970

Butchart, Harvey. *Grand Canyon Treks II.* La Siesta Press: Glendale, California, 1975.

Butchart, Harvey. *Grand Canyon Treks III.* La Siesta Press: Glendale, California, 1984.

Fletcher, Colin. *The Complete Walker III.* A.A. Knopf: New York, 1984.

Ganci, Dave. *Hiking the Southwest: A Sierra Club Totebook*. Sierra Club Books: San Francisco, 1983.

Grubbs, Bruce. *The Trail Guide to Northern Arizona*. Falcon Press. Helena, Montana, 1994.

Harmon, Will. *Wild Country Companion*. Falcon Press. Helena, Montana, 1994.

Heylmun, Edgar. *Guide to the Santa Catalina Mountains of Arizona*. Treasure Chest Publications: Tucson, Arizona, 1979.

Mazel, David. *Arizona Trails*. Wilderness Press: Berkeley, California, 1981.

Morris, Larry. *Hiking the Grand Canyon and Havasupai*. AZTEK Corp.: Tucson, Arizona, 1981.

Mitchell, James. *Fifty Hikes in Arizona*. Gem Guides Book Co.: Pico Rivera, California, 1985.

Nelson, Dick, and Sharon Nelson. *Hiker's Guide to the Superstition Mountains*. Tecolote Press: Glenwood, New Mexico, 1978.

Sheridan, Michael. *Superstition Wilderness Guidebook*. Sheridan Press: Phoenix, Arizona, 1971.

Thybony, Scott. *A Guide to Hiking the Inner Canyon*. Grand Canyon Natural History Association: Grand Canyon,

Arizona, 1980.

Wilkerson, James. *Medicine for Mountaineering*. The Mountaineers: Seattle, Washington, 1985.

FINDING MAPS

Arizona national forest and wilderness maps can be obtained from the United States Forest Service regional office at 517 Gold Avenue SW, Albuquerque, NM 87102. Local backpacking specialty shops often stock Forest Service maps.

Bureau of Land Management planimetric maps are similar to Forest Service maps but cover large areas of public land not included within national park or national forest boundaries. These maps are available from the United States Geological Survey.

Topographic maps published by the United State Geological Survey (NOT the U.S. Coast and Geodetic Survey) now cover nearly all of Arizona with varying degrees of accuracy and detail. Topos and state map indexes are available directly from the Survey at U.S. Geological Survey, Western Distribution Branch, Box 25286, Denver Federal Center, Denver, CO 80225. These maps are also available from many specialty backpacking shops as well as some general sporting goods stores and engineering supplies.

Getting it all together. A typical assortment of gear for an Arizona backpack trip. Bruce Grubbs

THE HIKER'S CHECKLIST

The following checklist certainly contains more items than any one hiker is likely to need; however, you may find it a useful reference in making sure that you have not forgotten anything essential. Remember to always have plenty of water and warm clothing. It is a good idea to have extra water in your vehicle, too.

Clothing

Shirt
Pants
Underwear
  (extras)
Windshirt
Vest
Belt and/or
  suspenders
Jacket or parka
Turtleneck
Poncho or rain suit
Gloves or mittens
Hat for sun
  and/or cold
Bandana
Walking shorts
Sweater
Swimming suit

Footwear

Boots
Socks
Boot wax
Moccasins or
  running shoes

Bedroom

Tent Poles
Tent stakes
Cord/guy lines
Fly Ground cloth
Sleeping bag
Sleeping pad or
  air mattress

Hauling

Backpack
Day or fanny pack

Cooking

Matches (extra)
Matches (waterproof)
Waterproof match case
Stove
Fuel bottles (filled)
Funnel Pad for stove

Cleaning wire for stove
Cleaning pad for pans
Fire starter
Cook kit
Pot gripper
Spatula
Cup
Bowl/plate
Utensils
Dish rag
Dish towel
Plastic bottle and/or
canteen

Food and drink

Cereal
Bread
Crackers
Cheese
Margarine
Powdered soups
Salt/pepper
Main course meals
Snacks
Hot chocolate
Tea
Powdered milk
Drink mixes

Photography

Camera
  Film (extras)
Extra lenses
Filters
Close-up attachments
Tripod
Lens brush/paper
Light meter
Flash equipment

Miscellaneous

Fishing gear
Pocket knife
Whetstone
Compass
Topo maps

Other maps
Sunglasses
Flashlight
Batteries (extra)
Bulbs
Candle
lantern
First aid kit
Snakebite kit
Survival kit
Repair kit
Sunscreen
Insect repellent
Toilet paper
Space blanket
Binoculars
Nylon cord
Plastic bags
Rubber bands/ties
Whistle
Salt tablets
Emergency fishing gear
Wallet/I.D. cards
Dimes for phone calls
Ripstop tape
Notebook and pencils
Field guides
Toothpaste
Dental floss
Mirror
Garbage bag
Book
Towel
Safety pins
Scissors
Trowel
Water purification system
Car key
Signal flare
Watch
Extra parts for stove,
  pack, and tent
Rubber tubing (to suck
  water out of shallow,
  rain-filled potholes)

THE AUTHORS

Stewart Aitchison is a guide for Lindblad Special Expeditions, Inc. and escorts travelers on natural history trips around the greater Southwest. He has written numerous articles and books about the area, including: *A Traveler's Guide to Monument Valley, Red Rock—Sacred Mountain: the Canyons and Peaks from Sedona to Flagstaff, A Wilderness Called Grand Canyon, A Guide to Exploring Oak Creek and The Sedona Area, A Naturalist's San Juan River Guide, A Naturalist's Guide to Hiking the Grand Canyon,* and *Utah Wildlands.* When not out exploring, he lives in Flagstaff, Arizona, with his wife, Ann, and daughter Kate.

Bruce Grubbs has been hiking, cross-country skiing, and climbing in the Southwest for more than twenty-five years. He has participated in several technical first ascents of peaks in the Grand Canyon, as well as numerous long backpack trips. He has explored most of Arizona's wilderness areas including many places which are not yet officially protected. He is the author of two other FalconGuides: *The Hiker's Guide to Nevada* and *The Trail Guide to Northern Arizona.* He has been a wildland fire fighter and a partner in an outdoor shop. At present, he is a charter pilot, computer consultant, writer, and photographer and is based in Flagstaff.

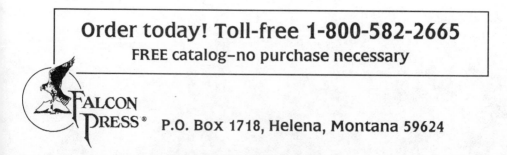

BRING ALONG A COMPANION

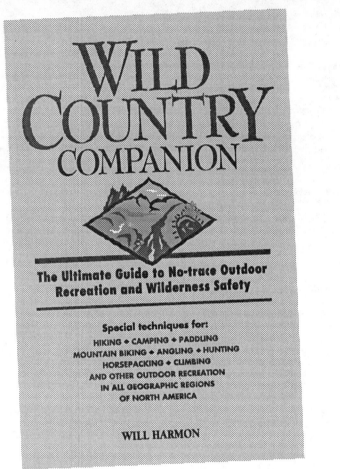

On your next trip to the great outdoors, bring along our FalconGuide, *Wild Country Companion*. Learn indispensable state-of-the-art methods for safe, no-trace traveling in North America's backcountry—whether you're on foot, bike or horse.

This guide was carefully compiled from recommendations by a range of experts including Forest Service researchers and managers, rangers, guides, and outdoor school instructors. It is packed with indispensible information on how to safely deal with hazards from bugs to bears and provides specific methods on different biome regions. There's also plenty of interesting anecdotes and illustrations.

As more and more people take to the outdoors, *Wild Country Companion* offers new ways to sustain our recreation resources. This book goes hand-in-hand with all our other FalconGuides and is a must for outdoor enthusiasts.

WILD COUNTRY COMPANION
By Will Harmon, Illustrated by Lisa Harvey
160 pp., 6 x 9", charts, softcover

For more information on this and other Falcon Press books visit your local bookstore.
Or call 1-800-582-2665

FALCO